MARTIN LUTHER KING, JR.

JACQUELINE L. HARRIS

MARTIN LUTHER KING, JR.

FRANKLIN WATTS
NEW YORK I LONDON I TORONTO I SYDNEY I 1983
AN IMPACT BIOGRAPHY

A GROLIER COMPANY

Cover photograph courtesy of
United Press International.
Photographs courtesy of:
United Press International: pp. 11, 57, 70, 85, 94, 99, 105;
Wide World: pp. 44, 104; Religious News Service: p. 67.

Library of Congress Cataloging in Publication Data

Harris, Jacqueline L.
Martin Luther King, Jr.

(An Impact biography)
Bibliography: p.
Includes index.
Summary: Describes the life, work, and
legacy of Martin Luther King, Jr.,
proponent of change through non-violence.
1. King, Martin Luther—Juvenile literature.
2. Afro-Americans—Civil rights—Juvenile literature.
3. Afro-Americans—Biography—Juvenile literature.
4. Baptists—United States—Clergy—Biography—
—Juvenile literature.   [1. King, Martin Luther.
2. Afro-Americans—Biography.   3. Civil rights] I. Title.
E185.97.K5H295 1983   323.4'092'4   [B] [92] 82-20099
ISBN 0-531-04588-9

CONTENTS

Dedicated to my mother
—The leader of the band is dead,
Her eyes are closed for good,
But her blood runs through my instrument,
And her song is in my soul—

Adapted from the lyrics of a song
by Dan Fogelberg

MARTIN LUTHER KING, JR.

"THERE IN MONTGOMERY LIVED A GREAT PEOPLE"

1

The place: Montgomery, Alabama
The date: December 1, 1955

Rush hour. People hurrying home. Horns honking. Brakes screeching. Buses nudging their way through traffic.

Making her way through the crowd of people at the bus stop in front of the Montgomery Fair department store was a woman who would make history today. She was Mrs. Rosa Parks, a black middle-aged seamstress. As the Cleveland Avenue bus rumbled to a stop, no one was happier to see it than Mrs. Parks. She was tired, her feet hurt, and she was burdened with a few Christmas gifts she had bought after work. A wisp of hair hung limply down from the circlet of braids pinned around the top of her head.

Pushing her way onto the bus, Mrs. Parks was lucky to find a seat in the fifth row. Contentedly she sank into the seat. How good it felt to rest her feet.

The bus driver edged the bus back into traffic. Two stops later, several white people boarded. There were no seats left. Montgomery law required that black people give up their seats to white people when the bus filled up. Several black people got up. But Mrs. Parks didn't move.

"Come on. Get in the back," said the driver. "Out of that seat!"

"No, I won't," said Mrs. Parks, peering up at the driver through her wire-rimmed glasses.

The driver just stared at Mrs. Parks. This polite lady was calmly defying him. And his bus was blocking the rush hour traffic. There was only one thing to do. The driver went for the police. He returned with two policemen, who led Mrs. Parks down the bus aisle and off to jail.

The other black passengers watched her sadly as she left. "Lawd, Lawd," said one black woman. She, like the other passengers, knew of the seven black passengers arrested for the same offense in the past year. One man had been shot to death by a bus rider for refusing to give up his seat.

For these people the pain of living life as a black person in Montgomery was routine. Blacks could not eat at a lunch counter or drink from a public fountain. Black people could not be served in turn in stores. They had to wait until all the white customers were served. Being black meant being called by your first name instead of being addressed as Mr. or Miss or Mrs. It meant segregation—separate waiting rooms in bus stations, separate schools, and separate lavatories. What the system said to black people was "You are less than . . . You are inferior." It hurt a lot. But it could hurt more to defy it. Mrs. Parks had defied it, and now she was in jail.

Mrs. Parks was charged with violating the city's segregation code. She called black community leader E.D. Nixon from jail. Nixon was president of the local chapter of the National Association for the Advancement of Colored People (NAACP) and headed another organization known as the Progressive Democrats. Nixon, a pullman porter, was deeply involved in the union activities of the Brotherhood of Sleeping Car Porters, headed by A. Philip Randolph.

Within hours, Nixon had arranged for Mrs. Parks' release on bail. The trial was set for the following Monday, December 5. The news of Mrs. Parks' arrest spread quickly through the black community. As neighbor told neighbor and friend told friend, an idea took shape—a brave idea, but a dangerous one. Nixon put it into words as he talked to his wife about Mrs. Parks' arrest. "I think every Negro in town should stay off the buses for one day in protest of Mrs. Parks' arrest." And so, with the leadership of Nixon, the Montgomery bus boycott was born.

Nixon spent the night calling the black leaders in Montgomery. His list included physicians, lawyers, teachers, business people, and union members. One person on his list was the new minister at the Dexter Avenue Baptist Church, Dr. Martin Luther King, Jr. This young minister was fresh out of Boston University. He was an excellent speaker and a minister who believed that part of being a good church member meant doing one's part for the community.

A meeting was called for the next day at Dexter Avenue Baptist Church. By 7 P.M., the time of the meeting, most of black Montgomery had heard that a bus boycott was being planned. Those attending the meeting quickly agreed to the boycott. Mrs. Jo Ann Robinson, an English professor and president of the Women's Political Council, had written a leaflet that would be printed and distributed. Dr. King promised to make thousands of copies on his church's mimeograph machine.

The leaflet read:

1. Another Negro woman has been arrested and put in jail because she refused to give up her bus seat.

2. Don't ride the bus to work, to town, to school, or anyplace on Monday, December 5.

3. If you work, take a cab, or share a ride, or walk.

4. Come to a mass meeting Monday, December 5, at 7 P.M. at the Holt Street Baptist Church.

One more problem remained to be solved—transportation for black people during the boycott. "I'm sure the black cab companies will agree to help out," said one minister.

By midnight, all the plans were made. The next day, Saturday, was a day of preparation. Leaflets were passed out. Cab companies were contacted. They agreed to take five passengers at a time and charge ten cents per person. Ministers prepared Sunday sermons in which they would urge their congregations to join the boycott.

The Sunday paper carried a front page story about the boycott. By Sunday afternoon, everyone in Montgomery knew that in protest of Mrs. Parks' arrest, black people would not ride the buses on Monday.

Dr. King rose early on Monday morning. His home was on the South Jackson Street bus route. This bus line carried more black people to work than any other. For a while he and his wife watched through the living room window for the first bus. Dr. King decided to get some coffee. While he was in the kitchen, he heard his wife call out, "Martin! Martin! Come quickly. It's empty! Empty!"

Indeed, a bus that was usually packed with black people was empty. The next bus was empty. The third bus carried two white people.

But what about the other bus lines? Dr. King backed his car out of the garage and rode up and down the bus routes. All in all, he counted only eight black bus passengers. At that time of the morning, buses were usually packed with black people. It's a miracle, he thought, as an empty bus went by.

Montgomery's black people had truly done it. They had stayed off the buses on December 5. Instead, they rode taxis or mules, and a few actually took a horse and buggy to work. Many walked—college students carrying heavy books, shoppers with packages, laborers carrying their lunch pails, housewives, clerks, maids, and plumber's helpers. Montgomery's black people were making history. One elderly woman, when asked if she wasn't tired of walking replied, "My feets is tired, but my soul is at rest."

December 5 was also the day of Mrs. Parks' trial. She was found guilty of violating Montgomery's bus segregation law that said there should be separate seating for white people and black people. Mrs. Parks was fined fourteen dollars and allowed to go home. Her lawyers promised to appeal this verdict to another court.

That afternoon Dr. King and other leaders of the boycott met. "Why not continue the boycott until the rules are changed?" suggested one minister.

"Even though black people stayed off the buses, still Mrs. Parks was found guilty," said another minister. "Let's suggest tonight that people stay off the buses until the bus company changes the unjust rules."

That day, an organization was born, the Montgomery Improvement Association (MIA). Dr. King was elected president. His first duty would be to address the mass meeting that night. Only the black people's response at the meeting could determine whether the boycott continued. Dr. King's speech would have to convince them.

People began gathering at 5 P.M. at Holt Baptist Church for the meeting. By 7 P.M., they filled the church and the streets for a block on all sides of the church.

After a prayer and the introduction of Mrs. Parks, Dr. King addressed the crowd. Loudspeakers carried his words to the people outside in the streets.

"We are tired—tired of being segregated and humiliated; tired of being kicked about by the brutal feet of oppression. . . . For many years we have shown amazing patience. We have sometimes given our white brothers the feeling that we liked the way we were being treated. But we come here tonight to be saved from that patience that makes us patient with anything less than freedom and justice. . . . One of the great glories of democracy is the right to protest for right. . . . We are protesting for the birth of justice in the community. . . . In our protest there will be no cross burnings. No white person will be taken from his home by a hooded Negro mob and brutally murdered. There will be no threats and intimidations. We will be guided by the highest principles of law and order. . . . We will only say to the [white] people, 'Let your conscience be your guide.' Love must be our regulating ideal. If we fail to do this, our protest will end up as a meaningless drama on the stage of history. . . . In spite of the mistreatment that we have confronted, we must not become bitter and end up by hating our white brothers.''

Booming through the chill December air, King's words seemed not to come from one person, but from all the people assembled—all the people who were ''tired of being segregated.'' Montgomery had a new leader. Black people everywhere had a new leader.

As Dr. King's words died away, another minister, Dr. Ralph Abernathy, rose to read the resolution prepared by the MIA. ''It is resolved that Negroes will not resume riding the buses until: 1. Courteous treatment of black people by bus drivers is guaranteed. 2. Passengers are seated on a first-come, first-serve basis, Negroes seating from the back of the bus, whites from the front of the bus. 3. Negro bus drivers are hired to drive black bus routes.''

''All in favor, stand,'' said Rev. Ralph Abernathy. They stood. They clapped. They cheered.

Black people of Montgomery would walk. They would stay off the buses until they could get better treatment on them. And so they walked and car-pooled and shared taxis all through December. MIA met twice with Montgomery city officials and representatives of the bus company. But there was no agreement.

At first the black boycott of buses was viewed with surprise and amusement by most white people. Weren't black people happy with their treatment on the buses? What made them think they could get along without them?

The car pools and the taxi arrangements and the walking went on. The loss of 17,500 black passenger fares and the loss of black business in the downtown area began to take a toll on Montgomery. After about three months, white businesses calculated that they had lost one million dollars. ''Settle this thing,'' they said to Montgomery city officials.

More meetings were held with the MIA. Once again the

MIA presented the demands agreed to at the mass meeting. The Montgomery officials argued that such demands were against the law.

"And besides," said the lawyer for the bus company, "if we grant Negroes these demands, they would go about boasting of a victory they had won over white people; and this we will not stand for."

To Dr. King, this statement revealed a great deal. He could see that the real problem was not buses or money or seats. It was the segregation laws—those which had been made to help keep blacks and whites apart. There were separate schools, separate waiting rooms, even separate drinking fountains. The separate facility set aside for Negroes was always shabbier. It seemed that the real purpose of segregation was to treat black people unjustly, to make them feel inferior. Thus, to say that black people were treated unjustly on the buses was unimportant to white officials. Justice had little to do with it as far as many white people in Montgomery could see. Segregation must continue.

A few white people raised their voices in protest. Mrs. Helen R. Gross wrote in a letter to the editor of the Montgomery paper, "I find it hard to believe that any fair-minded person can, under these circumstances, derive any pleasure from the comfort of having a seat while others who have paid the same fare are not allowed to occupy vacant seats merely because they happen to be a different race."

One white Lutheran minister, Rev. Robert Graetz, joined MIA; and another white Methodist minister, Rev. Glenn Smiley, came from Texas to lend his support to the boycott.

While many white people may have agreed with Mrs. Goss and the two ministers, they weren't brave enough to say so.

Through the month of January, the boycott continued. Neither side would give an inch. In frustration, whites tried a variety of tactics. City officials gave an interview to news reporters in which they said the boycott was settled. This trick would, they hoped, get the black passengers back on the buses. But MIA found out about the story before it got into print and passed the word in the black community that the boycott had not ended.

Car-pool drivers were threatened with the loss of their licenses and their insurance. Dr. King was arrested for driving 30 miles (48 km) an hour in a 25-mile (40-km) zone. But these tactics only strengthened the determination of King and the boycotters.

To some white people, the key to stopping the boycott was to stop Dr. King. He was the leader. His speeches and his example kept the boycott going. He was its inspiration.

Some tried to discourage King through the mail. Letters contained such messages as "You niggers are getting yourself in a bad place. The Bible is strong for segregation." Other crude and frightening letters were filled with curses and blasphemy. Some postcards read simply "Get out of town" and were signed KKK. The letters stand for Ku Klux Klan, an organization founded shortly after the Civil War. Its goal is to ensure that white Protestants dominate American society. Donning white hoods, the Klan rode out at night to terrorize black people. Their brutal acts against black people have included murder, beatings, and arson.

During the first three months of the boycott, Dr. King received at least one threatening phone call a day. One night he was awakened by the phone. A voice warned, "Listen, nigger, we've taken all we want from you. Before next week, you'll be sorry you ever came to Montgomery." For Dr. King, this call was the last straw. He got out of bed, went into the kitchen, and made a cup of coffee. Sitting over the coffee, he prayed, "God, I am afraid. I can't lead these people anymore." As he prayed, he felt new strength, a new courage. He would need that new strength a few days later.

On January 30, Dr. King's home was bombed. The bomb was thrown onto the front porch. Mrs. King heard the bomb strike the porch and wisely moved to the back of the house before the explosion. Dr. King was not there at the time, but he was quickly informed and rushed home. The street in front of Dr. King's house was filled with people. There were many

*Dr. Martin Luther King, Jr., urges
calmness after his home was damaged by a
bomb during the Montgomery bus boycott.*

angry faces in the crowd. Some had tears in their eyes. Some held guns. Others had bottles, broken to form dangerous weapons. Firemen were walking in and out of the smoke-filled house. Police stood on the porch and in the yard. Inside the house were the mayor and the police commissioner. King rushed through the crowd, past the people filling his home. There in the kitchen he found his wife holding their baby daughter. "Thank God," he said, holding them tightly.

The crowd outside began to shout insults at the police. Dr. King returned to the porch to face the angry crowd. "Please don't get panicky," he said. "My family is all right. Please go home. We cannot solve problems with violence. We must love our white brothers, no matter what they do to us. We must make them know we love them. Jesus still cries out across the centuries, 'Love your enemies.' That is what we must live by. We must learn to meet hate with love."

There was silence—not a cough, not a whisper from the crowd. Then someone sang out, "Amen." Another said, "God bless you, son." One by one the people drifted away.

The story of King standing on the porch of his bombed house, urging nonviolence, made the newspapers across the United States and in many foreign countries. Sympathy for the boycotters grew. Letters and donations poured into the MIA office from all over the world.

Still white Montgomery could not live with the demands of the black people. Perhaps segregation was unjust, but it was a way of life.

The Montgomery officials tried legal action. They charged Martin Luther King and eighty-nine other black people with interfering with a lawful business by organizing a boycott. Many times, MIA leaders had said in speeches, "It is an honor to face jail for a just cause." Now they would have a chance to live by these words.

The courtroom was packed during the trial. For four days, the defense lawyers brought in twenty-eight witnesses to tell about their experiences on buses. Bus rules required that a black person enter the front door of the bus, pay the fare, and then get off the bus and reboard through the side door. Many black witnesses had suffered because they obeyed this rule.

Mrs. Stella Brooks told the story of how her husband had been shot to death by police because he had demanded the return of his dime when the bus had been too crowded for him to board. Mrs. Delia Perkins had been called an ugly black ape by a bus driver. Another bus driver had driven off and left Mrs. Georgia Gilmore on the sidewalk after she had paid her fare and was walking to the side door of the bus.

Then Dr. King took the stand. He explained that black bus passengers could no longer endure the treatment they had received on the buses. The boycott was organized to protest this unfair treatment, and one main goal of MIA was to avoid violence.

But Dr. King had admitted organizing a boycott. The judge pronounced the eighty-nine people guilty of violating Alabama's antiboycott laws.

It was April. The boycott was four months old. People kept walking and car-pooling. Mass meetings were held to give the boycotters support and advice. Then the boycotters went to court. The NAACP and MIA filed a suit in a federal court asking that segregation be declared a violation of the Fourteenth Amendment of the Constitution. A three-judge panel heard the case on May 11. Lawyers for the city of Montgomery argued that desegregation of buses would cause bloodshed and violence between races.

"But," asked one judge, "is it fair to command one man to surrender his constitutional rights to prevent another from committing a crime?" After they heard both sides, the judges met to consider their verdict. About a month later, the verdict came. "The bus segregation laws of Alabama are unconstitutional." The city of Montgomery announced it would appeal the verdict to the Supreme Court.

Montgomery city officials went back to court with another suit. This suit charged that the MIA car pool was a public nuisance and an unlicensed private enterprise. If the city won this suit, the car pool, the main substitute for the buses, could not continue. It was the most serious threat to the boycott so far. Dr. King was afraid that without the car pool, people would gradually begin to ride the buses.

The trial took place on November 13. Halfway through the trial, Dr. King was handed a note by a reporter. It read, "The Supreme Court today affirmed a special three-judge U.S. District Court decision in declaring Alabama's state and local laws requiring segregation on buses unconstitutional." The highest court in the land had said segregation was unconstitutional!

The dispute that had shaken Montgomery for nearly a year was settled. The South would never be the same again. A way of life was about to disappear.

The night after the decision, the KKK formed a forty-car motorcade and drove along the main street of a black neighborhood. In the past, the sight of KKK white hoods and red badges had caused fearful black people to retreat to their homes and close the curtains. But this time porch lights went on and black people on the sidewalks waved to the hooded visitors. Embarrassed, the Klan motorcade turned up a side street and disappeared into the night. Indeed the South would never be the same.

The judge found the car pool illegal and ordered it disbanded. It was more than a month before the arrival of the federal order stating that Montgomery buses should be integrated. During that time, black Montgomery used share-the-ride arrangements, mules, or their own two feet to get around.

On December 21, 1956, the buses were integrated. Dr. King boarded a bus with Rev. Glenn Smiley. The two men, black and white, shared a seat in the front of the bus. It was 381 days after that fateful December 5, 1955, when the black people began to demonstrate their unwillingness to endure injustice any longer. Certainly they had fulfilled their hopes expressed by Dr. King during that first mass meeting at the Holt Baptist Church.

"There in Montgomery lived a great people—a black people—who injected a new meaning and dignity into the veins of civilization."

Some faced even more suffering after the buses were integrated. There were shootings and bombings. But after about a month, Montgomery was peaceful again.

Who was this Martin Luther King, Jr., who led the boycott? His words were golden. They inspired and uplifted people. How does such a man become a leader? The story of his growth from child to man helps us to understand.

GETTING SOME BIG WORDS

2

For twelve hours, the young Baptist minister had waited for the news. Now it came. He had a son. He jumped into the air and touched the ceiling in the hall.

The baby boy, born after a long labor, refused to breathe at first. But the doctor's slap on the baby's back forced air into the tiny lungs. And Martin Luther King, Jr., took his first breath. The date was January 15, 1929; the place, Atlanta, Georgia.

He will join me in the pulpit one day, thought the father as he held his baby son in his arms. Reverend Martin Luther King, Sr., was the pastor of Ebenezer Baptist Church in Atlanta.

The ministry was a destiny young Martin would find hard to avoid. His father and his grandfather before him had been Baptist ministers.

There was another destiny that the baby could certainly not avoid—growing up black in a society dominated by white people. It was a destiny that would be the source of much pain. The unfair treatment of black Americans cried out for justice. Something had to be done. In this, the baby's father and grandfather had provided a proud tradition for Martin to follow.

The Reverend Adam Daniel Williams, father of Martin's mother, had been the pastor of Ebenezer Baptist Church. Williams had lived through the 1906 Atlanta race riot. White mobs attacked black people, beating and killing many. He could remember peering through the living room curtains at white mobs moving down his street. It was a frightening experience, one that Rev. Adam Williams never really forgot.

Some years later, together with other black leaders, he formed a local chapter of the NAACP. This organization, founded in 1909, had as its goal the protection of the rights of black people. During the coming years, the NAACP would pursue the rights of black people in the courts. Laws would be changed and local officials would be ordered to obey those laws.

As one of its first acts, the new Atlanta NAACP chapter launched an attack on a city bond issue intended to provide money for new schools. Not one of those schools would be for black high school students. At that time there were no high schools for black students in Atlanta. The NAACP's efforts led to the building of Booker T. Washington High School in the mid-1920s. The NAACP members were called "dirty and ignorant" by *The Georgian*, the local newspaper. Williams organized a boycott of the newspaper. Six thousand black people canceled their subscriptions in one day. It was a severe blow to the paper, which eventually had to shut down its presses.

The baby's father, the Reverend Martin Luther King, Sr., was frequently called on to help his parishioners with problems. If someone couldn't find a job, needed a place to live, or was having trouble with the police or a bank, King found a way to help. He was an important member of the black community who knew many people. He was known as a "man who don't take no stuff." Thus, if someone was insulted by a clerk or had difficulty getting treatment at a hospital, King took quick action. He would march into the offending establishment and demand to see the person in charge. "I don't have time to waste," he would say. "Where's the top man's office?" Strong words for a black man in the South. But he was fearless. And he usually got results.

Rev. Martin Luther King led several organized efforts to right wrongs for black people in Atlanta. With his leadership, black teachers finally won the right to be paid the same as white teachers. He led the successful fight to integrate the Atlanta police force.

King, Williams, and other black leaders had helped to build a thriving black community in Atlanta. Black Atlanta boasted several black-owned insurance companies, banks, and construction companies as well as many other smaller businesses. The city would eventually have six black colleges. The black community had its own daily newspaper and radio station—the first black-owned media in the nation.

Within black Atlanta, by far one of the most flourishing black communities in the South, grew a tradition of black independence and self-confidence. This was the city where Martin Luther King, Jr., would grow into manhood.

Young Martin was the second child of Alberta and Martin Luther King, Sr. He had an older sister, Christine, and a younger brother, Alfred Daniel, whom everyone called A.D. The King children enjoyed a normal, happy childhood with bicycles, allowances, discipline, and much love.

As a young child, Martin quickly discovered the two things that would occupy most of his waking moments for the rest of his life.

Sitting in the front pew of his father's church and listening to his father preach, Martin discovered the power of words. As his father spoke, the people were moved. "Amen," they sang out. "Tell it, Reverend." The small boy had a good singing voice, and he learned many hymns in that front pew. His mother often took him to the church meetings where he had a chance to sing solos. His favorite hymn was "I Want to Be More and More Like Jesus." He'd take a deep breath and start. As he sang, his dark, earnest eyes would study the faces of his audience. The people were moved. He loved it. "Words! Someday I'm going to get me some big words," he would tell his mother on the way home.

He was six when he first found out about a cruel reality that, along with words, would dominate his life. His first playmates were two white boys, sons of the neighborhood grocer. In the South at that time, black children and white children often played together. But when the children started to school, white parents thought it best to discourage such friendships.

Martin thought nothing of the fact that he and his young white playmates went to different schools. But one day when he rang his playmates' doorbell, their mother told him, "Don't come around here anymore." "But why?" asked young Martin. "Well—uh—you can't play with the boys anymore. You can't—because you're colored and we're white." And then she closed the door.

Martin ran home to "Mother Dear," as he called his mother. She would explain this strange thing to him. What was colored? Was being colored bad? Was being white bad? Why was he colored? As these questions tumbled from the child's mouth, his mother took him on her lap and gave him a hug. Then she told him about how black people had been brought from Africa to America in chains. They had made the journey in crowded, dirty slave ships. Once there, they had been sold like cattle to white people. As purchased slaves, they had been forced to work without pay in fields, in homes, in shops, and in businesses. Sometimes their masters had been cruel, beating and insulting them. Some slaves had been lucky enough to have kind owners who treated them like part of the family. But still they had not been free, even though they deserved to be. The Civil War in America had freed the slaves. But white people would not accept black people as equals. They looked down on them and created a system that was nearly as bad as slavery; that system was segregation.

When his mother had finished speaking, the boy still did not really understand. "But why?" he asked. "Why do white people do this to us?" His mother could not think of an answer. She patted her son on the head, gave him a hug, and said, "Don't let this thing impress you. Don't let it make you feel you are not as good as white people. You are as good as anyone, and don't you forget it."

Those were words the child, the boy, and the man would never forget.

There were many times when young Martin saw his father put these words into action. Once, while driving along an Atlanta street, Martin's father went through a stop sign. A police car, lights flashing, siren screeching, pulled up alongside King's car.

"All right, boy, pull over, and let me see your license," shouted the police officer. King's face tightened with anger as he parked the car.

"OK, your license, boy," said the officer as he walked up to the car. King pointed to young Martin sitting beside him in the car. "This is a boy," he said quietly. "I am a man." It was a daring thing for a black man to say to a white police officer. Blacks sometimes suffered at the hands of the police. But the police officer simply looked at the black minister and said, "OK, you're a man. Now let me see your license."

On another occasion, young Martin was shopping for shoes with his father. They found some shoes in a store window that were just what Martin wanted. As the two entered, the clerk said, "You'll have to go to the back of the store before I can wait on you."

"We'll either buy the shoes right here in the front or we won't buy them at all," said King.

"There are no exceptions to this rule," said the clerk. "You take it just like everyone else, and stop being so high and mighty."

King looked down at his son and said, "We're leaving." He took Martin's hand and rushed out of the store. Martin had never seen his father so angry. "I will never accept this stupid, cruel system of segregation," muttered King. "I'll fight it until the day I die."

Martin was puzzled by segregation and frightened by his father's intensity. "I'll help you fight it, Dad," he said. "If you're against it, so am I."

"Thanks, Son," said the minister. He started the car and headed for home.

Martin did the usual things a boy does. He had a paper route. He had tussles and disagreements with his brother. But he refused to take on Black Billy, the school bully. He set up a soft drink stand on the lawn to earn spending money. Despite the fact that he was small, Martin went out for football. He played fullback, doggedly running over any opposing player in his path.

Martin was especially fond of his grandmother. Once when he sneaked out to watch a parade instead of doing his homework, he returned to hear the news that his beloved grandmother had died. He was convinced that his disobedience had caused his grandmother's death. In despair, he ran up the stairs and jumped out the bedroom window. He wasn't hurt, but he remained convinced that God was punishing the family for his disobedience.

His father talked to him the entire afternoon, trying to make Martin understand. "Don't blame what has happened to your grandmother on anything you've done. Death is a part of life that is hard to bear. God takes us when He's ready."

Martin's schooling was very important to him. For it was at school that he could "get some big words." After public school, he enrolled in Atlanta University's private laboratory school. From there, he went on to Booker T. Washington High.

In high school, he joined the debating team. His team was thoroughly beaten in its first debate. The defeat was made even more painful by something that happened during the bus ride home. When some white passengers got on the bus, the driver ordered the students to give up their seats.

When they hesitated, the driver cursed at them and called them niggers. They had to stand in the aisle for the entire 90-mile (144-km) ride.

One summer during his high school vacation, Martin, his brother, and several friends traveled north to Hartford, Connecticut, to work on a tobacco farm. It was Martin's first trip north. He marveled at the lack of "whites only" signs and the freedom to sit where you wanted on buses, in restaurants, or in movie theaters. But on the train trip back south, the students were made to sit in the back of the dining car behind a curtain. For Martin, this was a bitter pill. He felt as though "they had pulled down a curtain on my selfhood."

Though only a high school junior, he took and passed the entrance examination for Morehouse College. This Atlanta college had a fine reputation for training young black leaders of the South. Martin entered Morehouse in 1944. There he came under the guidance of professors who would eventually inspire him in the choice of his life's work.

So far Martin had resisted the pressure to enter the ministry. He felt that the foot-stomping, hand-clapping scenes in church were too emotional. The ministry should be more intellectual and thoughtful. People should be inspired to think. And above all, they should be inspired to play a role in making their community a better place to live. Hand-clapping had its place. But Martin Luther King, Jr., wanted to make a difference in people's lives. He wanted a career that would give him a chance to help people in a substantial way.

And so as Martin entered college, he signed up as a pre-med major. But not long after he began his courses in chemistry, physics, and biology, he discovered that he was just not suited for such a career. He changed his major to sociology, with the idea that he would eventually study law.

At Morehouse, Martin began a serious pursuit of the goal he had set as a small child. He set about to "get some big words." Martin began a determined effort to discover and understand the thoughts of the great philosophers of the world. He read about Moses, Socrates, Plato, and Aristotle.

From there he went on to Machiavelli, Descartes, Kant, Hegel, and Karl Marx. He read Henry Thoreau, finding the essay "On Civil Disobedience" especially interesting. Here was something he could compare to life as a black person in a white society. Thoreau contended that if you found a system to be evil, you should not accommodate your life to that evil system. He believed that one had a moral obligation to refuse to live in an evil system. And if you chose to violate an evil system, you had to pay the penalty society has designated. Thoreau spent a great deal of time in jail, opposing laws he thought were unjust. Certainly, thought King, Thoreau's thoughts could be applied to segregation laws.

As he read the great philosophers, Martin saw that their thoughts were an effort to relate human beings to the world they lived in. And that certainly was something he wanted to know more about.

Martin had an opportunity to learn more about blacks and the working world during his summer vacations. He worked as a stockroom helper at the Southern Spring Bed Mattress Company one summer. During another vacation, he took a job loading and unloading trains and trucks for the Railway Express Company. He learned that blacks were paid less than whites for the same work. Added to this were the daily abuses and indignities that some whites heaped on their black employees. When Martin's Railway Express foreman insisted on calling him "nigger," he quit. He didn't really need the money. As he left the Railway Express loading dock that day, his thoughts were of the blacks still working there. They did need the money. They had to stay and endure the unfair pay and the word "nigger." Martin's sociology professor's words took on even more meaning to him. "Money is not only the root of evil; it is also the root of this evil—racism."

Martin found the atmosphere at Morehouse freer. The school, supported by the American Baptist Convention, did not have to look to Georgia's power structure for support. Thus, the students were encouraged to discuss solutions to racial injustice. He could see that "no one there was afraid."

Students and professors could criticize the segregation system freely and could make their own proposals for what to do about it.

Martin found that many on the campus believed that black people represented a small nation within a larger one. He could not accept this idea. Black slaves had helped to build this country with their muscle and brains. And they deserved to be Americans in the fullest sense that the Constitution defined "American."

Daily attendance at morning chapel on the campus was required. But Tuesday morning chapel was special. For this was when the president, Dr. Benjamin Mays, spoke. Dr. Mays was an eloquent and stimulating speaker who was an inspiration to Martin. He could stir his audience and make them think.

Martin was also influenced by his religion professor, Dr. George Kelsey. Dr. Kelsey believed, as did Martin, that the minister's responsibility was to help parishioners find spiritual salvation and solutions to the everyday problems of life. "The good pastor," said Kelsey, "is also a good philosopher."

Martin understood that the hand-clapping was important as a way to forget one's troubles. But he believed that religion should guide one's mind and character.

During Martin's junior year at Morehouse, he realized that he wanted to be a minister. He told his parents of his decision. His father was delighted, but pretended to believe that Martin might not be able to preach. Could he stir people and hold their attention? King suggested a test sermon in one of Ebenezer's small meeting rooms. The trial sermon was announced. On the appointed Sunday, so many people crowded into the church that the minister was forced to move the event to the main sanctuary.

Seventeen-year-old Martin, wearing a white surplice, approached the pulpit and gave his first sermon. He spoke softly, not as dramatically as his father. He told the congregation about God and humanity and how they are related. He talked about human suffering and how it earned for humankind the peace and happiness of heaven. The shining faces of the congregation provided the verdict. Martin's first sermon was a huge success. He was ordained a minister in 1947 and was appointed assistant pastor of Ebenezer Baptist Church, his father's church.

Martin graduated from Morehouse in 1948. But he had just begun to learn how to think and to understand the great thinkers. He wanted to know more. He enrolled in Crozer Theological Seminary in Chester, Pennsylvania. There he began in earnest to search for a way to eliminate social evils. Now he was older and more mature. Philosophy took on a new dimension for him.

Slowly, as he pursued his studies at Crozer, Martin developed the justification and the means for opposing the unjust system of segregation and racial abuse. His beliefs were based on God. God, Martin believed, is the center of the universe. God is goodness and truth; therefore, all rules within the universe must be just and moral. Unjust rules must be changed, but only in ways acceptable to God. In other words, moral methods of change must be used. But what methods were these?

Martin searched his books and questioned his professors and fellow students for the answer to this question. Then one Sunday afternoon he attended a lecture given by Dr. Mordecai Johnson, a minister and president of Howard University in Washington, D.C. Johnson had just returned from India. During his visit, Dr. Johnson had learned a great deal about an Indian leader named Mahatma Gandhi. This man had used the power of love to help free India from British rule. This love is not the kind of love one has for a mother, a sweetheart, or a child. It is a brotherly love that recognizes we are all members in a community.

This brotherly love says to the person doing evil: Your evil hurts us all. If I react to your evil act with hate, you will respond with more evil. But if, instead, I meet your evil act with love, you are inspired to abandon your evil ways. Brotherly love stops evil in its tracks.

Gandhi's code of nonviolence had changed unjust laws in India. No matter what the British did to Gandhi and his followers, they did not react violently. They went to jail. They marched to the sea to make their own salt rather than pay an unjust British salt tax.

But that was India, where a large number of people opposed the unjust laws of a small white minority from another land. Would it work in America where the majority was white and the minority had once been enslaved? Martin wasn't sure.

Martin Luther King, Jr., graduated from Crozer in 1951 at the top of his class. He was awarded a scholarship, and he decided to use it to earn a Doctor of Philosophy degree at Boston University. In Boston he continued to explore the nature of God and the relationship of God and humanity. As he studied in Boston, he developed the beliefs that would guide him for his entire life. He came to believe that God is a part of all aspects of our lives and not a monarch who rules from afar. Martin's view of a personal God affirmed the dignity and worth of every human being, whether white or black, criminal or saint, idiot or genius, child or adult.

While he was in Boston, King met the woman he wanted to marry. She was Coretta Scott, a young music student from Alabama. She was not so sure she wanted to marry King. She didn't really like ministers. And besides, she had planned a career on the concert stage.

But he courted her, taking her to concerts and operas and to Boston's Western Lunch Box where Southern food was featured. And the day came when she knew she could not live without him. They were married on the lawn of her parents' home in Marion, Alabama, on June 18, 1953.

As his schooling drew to a close, King began to consider a number of positions. Because of his excellent academic record, he had plenty of offers to choose from, including dean of a college, teacher, and pastor of a church. Some of these positions were in the North, and some were in the South. He loved the South. But Coretta remembered the bitter experiences she had endured there. Her father's home and then his sawmill had been burned to the ground by white men carrying torches. Coretta had left the South, and she didn't want to return.

Martin's father expected him to return as co-pastor of Ebenezer Baptist in Atlanta. But Martin wanted his own church. And so in spite of his wife's desire to remain in the North, Martin accepted an offer made by Dexter Avenue Church in Montgomery, Alabama.

In May 1954 Dr. King was installed as pastor of Dexter. In that same month, the Supreme Court handed down a decision in the case of *Brown* v. *the Board of Education*. Brown was an eight-year-old black girl and the Board of Education was that of the city of Topeka, Kansas. The suit brought by the NAACP contested the Topeka Board of Education's refusal to allow the black girl to attend school with white children. The Supreme Court ruled that "in the field of education, the doctrine of separate but equal has no place. Separate educational facilities are inherently unequal." In other words, having separate schools for blacks and whites was unconstitutional. Black people read about the law. They realized that if separate schools were unconstitutional, so were separate restaurants, separate sections in trains, separate beaches, separate bus seating, and separate lavatories. It was unbelievable that the government had outlawed segregation. The North hailed the decision. The white South condemned it. Black Americans watched and waited. What would happen next?

It was in this atmosphere of watching and waiting that Rosa Parks refused to give up her seat on the bus. And the black people of Montgomery decided they were tired of the mistreatment they received at the hands of the bus company.

Dr. and Mrs. King had just settled down in the Dexter parsonage on Highland Avenue. Their first child, Yolanda Denise, was born in November 1955. They would eventually have three other children, Martin Luther, III, Dexter Scott, and

Bernice Albertine. Yolanda was just two weeks old when the call came from E.D. Nixon telling of Rosa Parks' arrest.

Dr. King was ready. He had read and he had studied. He had an idea—nonviolence.

TRIUMPH, TROUBLE, AND DEFEAT

3

In June 1957 Dr. King stood on the stage of the Morehouse auditorium. Nine years before, he had received his bachelor of arts degree. Now he was being awarded an honorary degree by Morehouse College President Benjamin Mays. Said Mays, "You are wiser at twenty-eight than most men are at sixty—living faith that most men preach about and never experience. You did not seek the leadership in the Montgomery controversy. It was thrust upon you. You led the people with quiet dignity, . . . Christian grace, and determined purpose. While you were away, your colleagues in the battle for freedom were being hounded and arrested like criminals. When it was suggested by legal counsel that you might stay away and escape arrest, I heard you say, 'I would rather spend ten years in jail than desert the people in this crisis.' At that moment, my heart, my mind, and my soul stood up erect and saluted you. I knew then that you were called to leadership for just such a time as this."

Dr. Mays might well have been speaking for a great many other people. Much had happened since December 1956, when blacks again boarded the buses in Montgomery.

Until Montgomery, black people had forgotten how to believe in themselves. But most had always had a strong religious faith. Dr. King took that faith and turned it into action. Together they had walked; together they had prayed; together they had faced up to an unjust system and had said "No more." And the system had fallen. Black people had come to believe in themselves after Montgomery. Life in America would never be the same again, for black people now knew it was possible to end segregation. Hadn't they done it in Montgomery? They would do it again.

For Dr. King, the leader who had inspired this great undertaking, the honors poured in. Other honorary degrees were awarded. At twenty-eight he was the youngest person ever to receive the Spingarn Medal, awarded by the NAACP to the person making the greatest contribution to race relations. He was invited to speak from the pulpit of such famous churches as the Cathedral of St. John the Divine in New York City. He spoke before the platform committee of the Democratic party. Articles in *Time* magazine and major newspapers spread the story of Dr. King and the Montgomery bus boycott to every corner of the nation.

Early in 1957 a southern black minister, Rev. C.K. Steele of Tallahassee, Florida, decided it was time for southern black ministers to meet and discuss what had been learned from Montgomery. The bus boycott in Montgomery had inspired a series of successful boycotts in Tallahassee, Atlanta, and several other southern cities.

At the meeting the ministers decided to ask President Dwight Eisenhower to make a speech in the South urging officials to abide by the 1954 Supreme Court decision. Certainly this would speed the integration of blacks and whites. They also decided to ask that Vice-President Nixon tour the South and meet with black and white leaders. In addition, they requested that the Justice Department make a study of the South's peculiar problems. The letters were sent to Washington. Shortly afterward, the answers came back. "No time." "Not convenient now."

Undaunted, the ministers held another meeting in New Orleans. More than a hundred ministers attended. They formed an organization that they named the Southern Christian Leadership Conference (SCLC). Dr. King was elected president. SCLC voted to ask Washington for a White House conference on civil rights. Back came the response, "Not a good time for this."

Dr. King, by now exhausted from the Montgomery boycott and what had followed, decided to accept an invitation to attend the Independence Day celebration of the African country of Ghana, which was gaining its independence from Great Britain. Dr. and Mrs. King joined a party of prominent black Americans on the journey to Ghana. As he stood watching one flag go down and another go up, Dr. King felt a special pride and happiness for the black African country.

While in Ghana, the Kings met Vice-President Nixon who invited them to visit him in Washington. That was one invitation Dr. King intended to accept; SCLC had an urgent need to talk to Washington. However, what was really needed was a White House civil rights conference.

On his way home, King stopped in New York City to help plan a dramatic appeal to Washington. He discussed the idea with two black leaders, A. Philip Randolph, head of the Brotherhood of Sleeping Car Porters, and Roy Wilkins, national president of the NAACP. Later, in a meeting with seventy other civil rights leaders, the Prayer Pilgrimage was planned.

On May 17, 1957, approximately thirty-seven thousand people, black and white, gathered in front of the Lincoln Memorial to demonstrate their support of the Supreme Court decision. Many black leaders, including Dr. Mordecai Johnson, Roy Wilkins, and A. Philip Randolph, spoke to the crowd. Dr. King was the last to speak. He called upon all branches of the government to encourage and pursue desegregation. The White House's support of desegregation has been "silent and apathetic," he said. Pointing out that in many parts of the South blacks were denied their voting rights by intimidation, poll taxes, and other devices, King asked for a change in this unfair system. "Give us the ballot," he said. "We will no longer plead . . . we will write the proper laws . . . we will fill the legislature with men of good will . . . we will get the people judges who love mercy."

In an effort to get the ballot, SCLC organized the Crusade for Citizenship. The goal was to register five million southern black voters, but to many people this was unrealistic. They knew about the long list of questions, long lunch breaks, coffee breaks, long phone calls, bad information, and all the other time-consuming ways white registrars had to discourage the black person waiting to register to vote.

Vice-President Nixon could scarcely ignore the words spoken at the Lincoln Memorial. Six days later, he offered to meet with King. At the meeting, King asked for help and support in the civil rights cause. He asked that the president and vice-president make speeches to support the constitutional rights of black people. But Nixon made no promises. King left empty-handed.

In the fall of 1957 Congress passed the first civil rights bill since 1875. The bill created a Civil Rights Commission which had the authority to investigate voting irregularities. But it was a weak bill that would have little effect on black voter registration. What was needed was supervision of voter registration by federal marshals.

In June 1958 President Eisenhower finally agreed to meet with King and three other black leaders. The president listened politely to the nine-point proposal presented by the group. Basically the program asked the president to take the lead in supporting civil rights and in finding a way to bring the races together in peace. Laws were needed, the proposal said, to ensure the rights of black people. Black people should be given protection so they could vote. Bombings, beatings, and murders of black people should be investigated by the Federal Bureau of Investigation.

Eisenhower replied to the proposal by sadly shaking his head. "There are so many problems—Lebanon, Algeria. . . ." So many problems in other countries struggling to right their internal wrongs, thought King, and no time to help black Americans gain the rights guaranteed them by the Constitution.

The president spoke of how complex race relations were. Laws would not help, he said. People's hearts must change. And so King again left the White House empty-handed.

Four times in a year and a half, King had asked the White House for support. "No time." "Not a good time." A handshake; a sad shake of the head. These had been the answers. Eisenhower feared losing southern votes in Congress. Without southern support he would have trouble promoting new laws in Congress. Nixon, who hoped to succeed Eisenhower in the White House, feared that losing the southern vote would cost him the election.

And so Dr. King went back to Atlanta to continue the struggle on his own.

King had just finished writing a book, *Stride Toward Freedom*, describing the Montgomery bus boycott. The book would, he hoped, spread the word about the plight of the black people and their struggle for civil rights. In the fall of 1958 he traveled north to promote the book. He appeared on TV and gave radio interviews. He also went to stores where the book was on sale and autographed copies for customers. King was cheered in Detroit and Chicago. But there were also "boos" from the crowds. In New York City, his reception was even less friendly. At one point his car was pelted with eggs. He appeared at a rally in Harlem where he chided a new black group called the Black Nationalists for advocating violence.

Later that afternoon, King went to Blumstein's department store in Harlem to autograph copies of his book. As he sat down at the desk, the customers lined up to take their turn. A dark-skinned heavy-set woman pushed her way past the line to the desk. "Are you Mr. King?" she asked. "Yes, I am," he said, smiling.

The woman began to curse. "Luther King," she screamed, "I've been after you for years." Then she took a letter opener from her purse and plunged it deep into King's chest. She turned and tried to run from the store, but store employees stopped her.

King remained conscious and upright in his chair, the handle of the blade protruding from his chest. Someone wanted to remove the letter opener. "No," said one man, "let the doctors do it."

The police and an ambulance were called. At the hospital surgeons removed the blade successfully. Dr. King spent ten days in the hospital. But a bout with pneumonia complicated his recovery; it was four months before he was completely well.

King's attacker, forty-two-year-old Isola Curry, was questioned by the police. Why did she attack King? "He's trying to convert me from being a Roman Catholic." "He's a communist; the FBI is checking on him." "People are torturing me."

"The woman is ill," said the judge at her hearing. She was sent to a hospital for the criminally insane.

During his convalescence, King had a lot of time to think and read. Having experienced violence firsthand, he wanted to visit the land of the man who had inspired his belief in nonviolence. Perhaps he could learn more about how Gandhi had inspired nonviolence in his followers.

On February 10, 1959, King finally set foot on Indian soil, the land of Gandhi and nonviolent protest. "To other countries I may go as a tourist, but to India I come as a pilgrim," he said to the officials who met his plane.

King met Indian Prime Minister Pandit Nehru. He was impressed with Nehru's determined effort to halt the oppression of the untouchables, or outcasts, of Hindu society. They had been discriminated against for centuries. King could not help but compare Nehru to Eisenhower, who he felt had turned a deaf ear to black pleas for civil rights.

King spoke to people who had worked with Gandhi, and he visited Gandhi's shrine. He became more certain that nonviolence was the only way to oppose injustice. As he wrote in a letter shortly before he left for India, "The Negro all over the

South must come to the point that he can say to his white brother, 'We will match your capacity to inflict suffering with our capacity to endure suffering. We will meet your physical force with soul force. We will not hate you, but we will not obey your evil laws. We will soon wear you down by pure capacity to suffer.' " And King knew that black people could do it.

His thoughts turned to the thousands of black people in Montgomery who walked as much as 12 miles (19 km) back and forth to work every day for a year rather than endure the humiliation of segregated buses.

Leaving India, King returned to a country where the seeds of black hope were beginning to sprout. Here and there a city was locked in a struggle with its black citizens over segregation. But for every such city, a dozen were quietly dropping their segregation laws.

Small steps had been taken since the Montgomery victory. Black voter registration was rising slowly. But the slow progress wasn't enough for black people. Their hopes were high. They had gotten a taste of their rights, and they wanted them all—now.

There were many setbacks. In April 1959 a black man, Mack Parker, was lynched by a white mob in Mississippi. Black people across the country called for the punishment of his killers. One Virginia county, rather than integrate its schools, dissolved the public school system. The White House's silence continued. Dr. King wrote to the attorney general to protest the discrimination at a government missile site in Alabama. He got a polite "thanks for your letter," but no results.

New black voices, born of the frustrated hopes, were heard. Black Muslim leader Elijah Muhammad and his young assistant, Malcolm X, urged blacks to hate the "blue-eyed devils."

King realized that the struggle for civil rights had reached a crisis. Black hopes were high, and blacks seemed to be on the verge of mounting a violent struggle to gain those rights. King knew that black people as a minority couldn't win in a violent battle with the majority. Only by acting together in organized masses on the march could black people exert power. Defeating such resistance would be much more difficult than defeating a small band of armed black people. Gandhi had said to his followers, "Never let them rest. Our powerful weapons are the voices, the feet, and the bodies of dedicated united people moving toward a just goal."

King realized that he must devote more time to SCLC. He decided to resign from his pastorate at Dexter Avenue Church and move to Atlanta. There he could work with his father at Ebenezer Baptist Church. As co-pastor, he would have more time for SCLC.

While King settled down in Atlanta, another seed of his efforts sprouted in Greensboro, North Carolina. Two college students, Ezell Blair and Joseph McNeill, inspired by the Montgomery bus boycott, decided they had had enough of segregated lunch counters. "Let's have a boycott," said McNeill. The next day, they and two other students went to a downtown Woolworth store and sat down at the lunch counter.

"We won't serve you," said the man behind the counter. Still they sat. They remained at the lunch counter for two and a half hours. For the next three days, they came and sat at the counter. On the fourth day white students from a nearby women's college joined them. The white students refused to order unless the black students were served.

The lunch counter sit-ins made the headlines. Black students and white students started sit-ins in Durham and in Winston-Salem. After two weeks, ten student sit-ins were in progress in North Carolina, and the movement had spread to three neighboring states. Two months later, sit-ins were in progress in fifty southern cities.

The students followed King's advice about nonviolence. They sat peacefully at counters while white hecklers poured catsup on their clothes and salt on their heads. In Orangeburg, South Carolina, police threw tear gas at students gathering outside a restaurant, and then firemen turned their fire hoses on the students. The tremendous force of the water knocked the students to their knees. Wet and shivering, they were then hauled off to jail.

SCLC offered the students advice and support. A special student meeting was arranged for April 1960 in Raleigh, North Carolina. More than two hundred people attended. At the meeting the students organized the Student Nonviolent Coordinating Committee (SNCC). At the end of the meeting, they joined hands and sang "We Shall Overcome." This hymn was to become the special song of the movement.

King and his brother joined students in a sit-in at a department store in Atlanta. They were jailed with the students. With the exception of King, all were later released. In King's case, the judge ruled that his participation in the sit-in had violated parole granted after conviction for a traffic violation. King was sentenced to four months of hard labor at Reidsville State Prison. The judge's verdict was openly condemned by an Atlanta newspaper. The Justice Department pressured President Eisenhower to secure King's release, but the president did nothing.

It was an election year. Senator John Kennedy and Vice-President Richard Nixon were the leading candidates for president. Kennedy's brother Robert called the judge and asked about King's constitutional right to bail. John Kennedy called Mrs. King and offered his sympathy and support. The next day, the judge granted King bail. King was free. The Kennedys' support for King is credited with influencing enough votes to win Senator Kennedy the election by a narrow margin.

The sit-ins continued through 1960 and into 1961. Students on northern campuses supported the effort with petitions, fund raising, and picketing. By the fall of 1961, seventy thousand people, black and white, had taken part in sit-ins in a hundred cities. Lunch counter segregation had been abolished in twenty-seven southern cities.

The success of the sit-ins inspired young black students. They developed a pride in being black, a pride symbolized by soul music and Afro haircuts. As they participated with white

Arrested for demonstrating to protest
lunch counter segregation, Dr. Martin Luther
King, Jr., walks to jail alongside another
demonstration leader, Lonnie King.

students in sit-ins, blacks learned that many white people were opposed to the evils of segregation.

In the spring of 1961, SCLC, SNCC, and the Congress on Racial Equality (CORE) decided on a unique way to spread the sit-in movement throughout the South. Sit-ins would go "on the road." Black and white volunteers would ride buses from town to town, stopping to sit in at lunch counters and to use segregated lavatories and waiting rooms.

The Freedom Riders, as they came to be known, encountered some of the worst violence seen during the entire sit-in campaign. When one Freedom Ride bus arrived in Anniston, Alabama, an angry mob smashed the bus windows and slashed the tires. Then the mob threw an incendiary bomb through a window, setting the bus afire. As the Freedom Riders got off the burning bus, they were beaten.

A mob in Birmingham, Alabama, hauled Charles Person, a black student, and James Peck, a white student, off a bus and into an alley and beat them. Screaming "nigger-lover" at Peck, they beat him so badly that it took fifty-three stitches to close the wounds in his face. Newspapers throughout the country carried photos of Peck being beaten and of his bleeding face. Birmingham was ashamed. "It will take us a long time to live this down," said one Birmingham business leader.

In many cases during these attacks police stood by and did nothing. Sometimes the medical needs of the injured were ignored. In Montgomery, a white student whose front teeth had been kicked in lay on the ground in a semiconscious condition for an hour. A reporter suggested to a police official that the student needed an ambulance. "He hasn't requested one," was the reply. Only when the MIA sent cars did he get the medical attention he needed.

At the height of the violence in Montgomery, two Freedom Riders were saved from further beating and possible death by one courageous Alabama official on the scene. He was Floyd H. Mann, the state public safety director. He pushed his way through the mob and pulled out his revolver, screaming "Stop the beating!" This brave man was later fired.

The violence in Montgomery continued throughout the day. One Freedom Rider was soaked with gasoline and set afire.

King held a rally that night in a Montgomery church. A stone-throwing mob gathered outside. It took the National Guard and federal marshals most of the night to disperse the mob. Inside the church, the people joined hands and sang "We Shall Overcome" and other songs and hymns.

Why had Alabama been so vicious to the Freedom Riders? King blamed Governor John Patterson, who a few days before had said, "The people of Alabama are so enraged that I cannot guarantee protection for this bunch of rabble-rousers." Indeed, the volatile feelings seemed to be contagious.

"The law may not be able to make a man love me, but it can keep him from lynching me," said King in response.

The Freedom Riders helped to spread the word of the viciousness of segregation. The nation's conscience was stirred. A new message went up in buses, bus stations, and on bus tickets. The message was "Service must be rendered without regard to race, color, creed, or national origin by order of the Interstate Commerce Commission."

One Freedom Ride into Albany, Georgia, became the basis of an SCLC campaign that ended in failure. The segregated town had been the scene of much trouble. Black servicemen from nearby army bases and students from the small local college were especially harassed by discrimination.

King began a series of mass marches, boycotts, and prayer vigils in Albany. Albany's response was to arrest everyone and then let them go. There was little publicity to arouse the nation's conscience. Because of the campaign, many black people lost their jobs, four black churches were burned to the ground, and Albany remained much the same as it had been. It would take the Civil Rights Act of 1964 to desegregate Albany.

Mounting an all-out attack on the segregated system without a clear plan had been a mistake. A clear-cut goal, with well-planned ways to achieve that goal, was required.

King had learned a lesson that would serve him well. Instead of attacking the entire system of segregation in Albany, one or two goals of desegregation should have been set—desegregation in jobs and on buses, for instance. The strengths of the black community of Albany had been poorly assessed. For example, a boycott of white businesses was organized when, in fact, black people seldom shopped in white business establishments.

King had relied on his ability to move people to action. Now he realized that even a natural leader needed a good plan.

BIRMINGHAM IS THE TARGET

4

With the painful lessons of Albany still fresh in his mind, King began planning another campaign in early 1962. The target this time would be the city of Birmingham, which had been called the "most thoroughly segregated big city in the United States." King was certain a victory in Birmingham would benefit the entire nonviolent movement in the South. He believed that "as Birmingham goes, so goes the South."

Certainly Birmingham was a challenge for King. "It's so nice to have you in Birmingham" read large signs along the main streets of the city. But the signs had little meaning for most black residents of the city in 1962. Black people were restricted to menial, low-paying jobs. Despite the fact that desegregation was taking place throughout the South, segregation in Birmingham was total—in the schools, churches, restaurants, hospitals, and theaters. The city had closed down its public parks, libraries, and bus lines rather than integrate them. Birmingham had given up its professional baseball team rather than allow its all-white team to play against integrated opposing teams. Black people who chose to challenge segregation were often beaten or killed. In the previous six years, there had been seventeen bombings of black churches and homes. All had gone unpunished. There had been fifty incidents of cross burnings on the lawns of black residents. Blacks were routinely beaten by police or arrested without reason.

Perhaps no one embodied Birmingham's cruel system of segregation better than Eugene "Bull" Connor, the Commissioner of Public Safety. A year before, he had arrested the manager of the bus terminal four times in two weeks for complying with the bus desegregation order issued by the Interstate Commerce Commission. Some claimed that Connor had threatened business people who wanted to remove "white only" and "colored only" signs from their premises. He was often heard to say he had to "keep the nigger in his place."

In the fall of 1962 King began planning in earnest for the Birmingham campaign. A three-day conference of SCLC staff was called at an SCLC educational center near Savannah, Georgia. King was determined to put the lessons learned in Albany to work in Birmingham. These lessons included focusing on one target and making careful plans. The target in Birmingham would be the one area that was not segregated—the downtown stores. Black people were free to shop at any counter in any store, but they were required to try on clothes in special fitting rooms and to drink from "colored only" drinking fountains. Blacks would boycott all downtown businesses.

The Birmingham campaign was given the code name Project C, for Project Confrontation. Careful plans were made at the Savannah meeting to solve any possible problem. King would go on a fund-raising tour to raise money for bailing out those who were arrested. Speeches and meetings in the Birmingham area would gain support for the SCLC and its nonviolent methods. The campaign would begin with small demonstrations and build gradually to large demonstrations. There would be no letup. Day by day, the effort would grow. Project C would begin just before Easter in order to have a significant impact on the pre-Easter shopping business. A command post for Project C was set up in Room 30 of the A. G. Gaston Motel in Birmingham. SCLC staff members made a careful study of downtown Birmingham, noting locations of key businesses, landmarks, entrances to stores, lunch counters and the number of seats at each counter. This information would allow the rapid dispatching of demonstrators to important locations.

Project C began on April 3, 1963. A manifesto was issued that listed the grievances of black people and announced the beginning of a campaign to protest these wrongs. The manifesto read in part: "The patience of an oppressed people cannot endure forever. . . . We have been segregated racially, exploited economically, and dominated politically. . . . We sought relief by petition for the repeal of city ordinances requiring segregation . . . but the city had callously refused to yield our basic rights. . . . Open protest is the sole meaningful alternative. . . . We act today in full concert with the law of morality and the Constitution of our nation. The absence of justice and progress in Birmingham demands that we make a moral witness to give our community a chance to survive."

The campaign began on that same day with picketing and sit-ins involving thirty black people. The twenty demonstrators who sat in at a department store lunch counter were arrested. Other smaller groups were not arrested, but the lunch counters were shut down. Five hundred people attended the rally held that night. "We are headed for freedom land," King told the crowd, "and nothing is going to stop us."

During the rest of the week, several more small sit-ins took place. On April 6 forty-two demonstrators marched silently in two-by-two formation toward city hall. Three blocks from city hall they encountered a row of Birmingham police. The police ordered the marchers to disperse. The marchers refused politely, and the police politely arrested them. The next day, Palm Sunday, twenty-five marchers taking part in a prayer march were arrested. During this time, the police, at Bull Connor's direction, had been unusually polite to the black demonstrators. Connor knew that the city was in the process of having an injunction issued by the court to ensure public safety by prohibiting any more demonstrations. He knew that King had never violated a law, and he believed that King would certainly not violate an injunction.

The injunction was issued on Wednesday, April 10. Disobeying unjust laws and court orders had been much on King's mind since he had read Thoreau. He believed that laws are made to ensure justice, and to make it unlawful for black people to demonstrate in order to obtain their constitutional rights was unjust. Of course, as Thoreau had written, the person who violated what he considered to be an unjust law must stand ready to pay the penalty set forth by society for violating that law. It was clear to King that the injunction must be violated. The demonstrations would continue.

At a mass meeting on Wednesday night, King announced that the injunction had been delivered. He explained that it meant anyone demonstrating in the future would be violating a court order and could be arrested. "But," he said, "it's better to go to jail in dignity than accept segregation in humility." King planned to lead a demonstration on Friday, Good Friday. His friend Rev. Ralph Abernathy and the singer Al Hibbler had promised to join him. "We are going to have to keep alive this activity until the power structure says, 'These people really mean business.' " He urged everyone to continue the boycott of downtown businesses. "Any Negro who is walking downtown these days with a package is not fit to be free," he said.

Ralph Abernathy was the next speaker at the meeting. "Who'll volunteer to go to jail with me and Martin and Al Hibbler?" Hands went up, and fifty volunteers were recruited. "I've never been to jail in my life," said an elderly woman, "but I'm going too." As one, the entire audience rose to their feet singing "I'm on my way to freedom land!"

On Good Friday, King, Abernathy, and Hibbler led the march from the Sixth Avenue Zion Church toward the city's downtown section. Singing hymns as they went, the demonstrators were cheered by a thousand black people lining their route. As the marchers passed, the onlookers shouted, "Freedom has come to Birmingham!" Some fell to their knees in prayer. When the marchers had covered eight blocks, Bull Connor decided he had had enough. "Stop them!" he shouted to the police officers. The officers, hearing the angry tone of Connor's voice, grabbed the marchers roughly and dragged them into the waiting police vans. They were taken to jail. King was put in solitary confinement.

Alone in his cell, he worried about the others. Were they all right? Would there be enough bail money to get everyone out? He worried about his wife, who had just given birth to their fourth child. He felt cut off from the world. Even the sunlight did not penetrate his dark cell. Finally, on Saturday, he was permitted to have visitors.

On Sunday, which was Easter, the focus of the campaign was on church and prayer. Six groups of two or three black people each sought to worship at six white churches. Two of the churches welcomed the black people and invited them to return. At a third, the visitors were invited to pray with the church elders at the parish house. But the other three churches refused admission to the black people. "Go to the colored church," said one usher, barring the church door. "White people built this church and white people worship here."

That afternoon, King's brother, Rev. A.D. King, wearing his minister's surplice and carrying a Bible, led twenty-eight marchers toward the city jail. He wanted to lead prayers there for his brother and the 150 others in jail. They had gone only a few blocks when they were arrested. The police called for vans to take the demonstrators to jail. As they waited, a crowd of angry black people gathered. They began to shout that the marchers should not be arrested. After the police van had taken away the marchers, the police turned their attention to the onlookers. When they tried to arrest one woman, the crowd began to throw rocks at the police. The police responded with their nightsticks, and it seemed as if a riot was about to occur. But police reinforcements arrived with dogs, and the crowd broke up quickly.

Dr. King's arrest opened the way for negotiations with the black demonstrators. Black and white ministers began talks with SCLC staff members, the interracial Alabama Council on Human Relations, local business people, and the mayor. Although the meetings did produce a plan for granting the blacks' demands, the negotiators needed the approval of the larger business community.

Several ministers criticized King's campaign as "unwise and untimely." They said they understood the "natural impatience" of black people, but the demonstrations were causing "racial friction and unrest." They urged the black community to withdraw its support of the demonstrations, which they said were led by "some of our Negro citizens and in part by outsiders."

King wrote a reply to this criticism from his cell. "My dear Fellow Clergymen," the nine-thousand-word letter began. It went on to answer the ministers' statements point by point. In part, the letter said, "I have yet to engage in a direct-action campaign that was well-timed in the view of those who have not suffered unduly from the disease of segregation. For years now I have heard the word, 'Wait!' It rings in the ear of every Negro with piercing familiarity. This 'wait' has almost always meant 'never.' . . . We have waited for more than 340 years for our constitutional and God-given rights. . . . Perhaps it is easy for those who have never felt the stinging darts of segregation to say 'wait,' but when you have seen vicious mobs lynch your mothers and fathers . . . when you have seen hate-filled policemen curse, kick, and even kill your black brothers and sisters . . . then you will understand why we find it difficult to wait."

King in his jail cell
in the Jefferson County
Court House in
Birmingham, Alabama.

A few days after Easter, King, Abernathy, and some of the others in jail were bailed out. They went directly to their Gaston Motel headquarters to plan their next move. After a long meeting, they decided to recruit black schoolchildren to march in a huge demonstration. Volunteers went into class-rooms and libraries to recruit children ranging in age from six to sixteen. The young recruits were shown films about SCLC efforts in other areas. They were given lessons in nonvio-lence, what it meant, and how important it was. Within two weeks, a six-thousand-member children's crusade was ready to march.

The first group of three hundred children met at the Six-teenth Street Baptist Church on May 2. There they had lunch and received instructions from King and other SCLC staff members. To the cheers of black onlookers, a group of thirty-eight children set off toward downtown. Holding hands and singing "We Shall Overcome," the children marched just two blocks before they were arrested. Then another group marched out of the church, and another. As soon as one group was arrested, another group moved out. More children arrived at the church to take their turns in the march.

When the police approached to arrest them, a few chil-dren ran away. But most, as they had been instructed, dropped to their knees in prayer. So many children were arrested, the police quickly ran out of police vans to transport the children to jail and had to call up school buses. A total of 959 children were arrested that day.

King was criticized for risking the lives of children. His reply was to ask where these concerned people were when the children had first felt the pain of discrimination—when they had turned to their mothers, as he had done, and had asked, "Why, Mama, why?" He wanted to involve the children in the struggle to make the world they were growing up in a better place.

The next day, the children gathered to march again. They left the church chanting "We want freedom!" The police were out in force, and they moved in to block the path of the marchers. The children were ordered to stop. "Freedom," came the reply from a line of six-year-olds. "We want freedom!" echoed the others. The children kept marching. For Bull Connor, that was enough. "Turn on the water," he shouted. The high-pressure water from the fire hoses surged into the crowd of marching children, throwing them to the pavement, actually tearing the clothes off some. As they tried to get up, they were knocked down again by the powerful streams of water.

Angered by the sight of the children being treated so brutally, one group of adult onlookers launched a barrage of rocks, bottles, and bricks at the police. Then the police dogs were unleashed and allowed to attack the crowd. Snarling and flashing their teeth, the dogs tore at clothing and flesh. At least three children were seriously bitten.

The battle with rocks, water, and dogs raged for more than two hours. When it was over, many of the marchers were badly bruised, and several firemen and a reporter had been hurt by bricks. Through it all, the news cameras had been at work, and the next day all of America saw what had happened in Birmingham that afternoon. One photo showed police officers holding a teenaged boy while a dog ripped off his sweater. Other photos showed fire hoses being trained on six- and seven-year-olds. America was horrified, and Birmingham was ashamed.

Several days later, with comedian Dick Gregory in the lead, the children marched again. Again, as group after group marched up to the police lines, they were arrested. Now the jails were full. The next day, as the children began their march, the police simply broke up their lines and scattered them. When the people in the Sixteenth Street Baptist Church saw this, they came out. "If they're not going to arrest our marchers, let's all go downtown," said one of the SCLC leaders. And so, moving by different routes and gathering others as they marched, more than three thousand black people poured into the downtown area. Once there, they moved in and out of stores, singing "Ain't gonna let nobody turn me 'round—I'm on my way to freedom land." Then they returned to the church and set off again for the downtown area.

The sight of these demonstrators swarming through the streets frightened many of the business people. Said King, "There were Negroes on the sidewalks, in the streets, standing, sitting in the aisles of downtown stores. There were square blocks of Negroes, a veritable sea of black faces." The unnerved business people found it hard to think of anything but the demands of black people for their rights.

As the marchers returned to the church, intent on marching downtown again, they were met by police, who herded them into a nearby park. The crowd shouted at the police, and the fire hoses were turned on again. Once again the bricks and rocks flew. The battle raged for an hour and a half. Finally, the blacks retreated to the church, throwing rocks as they went. Firemen trained their hoses on the church, shattering stained-glass windows. Inside, the SCLC staff lectured the people on nonviolence, pointing out that rock-throwing would hurt the cause. At least twelve people were hurt, but there were few arrests.

By now Birmingham was making the headlines all across the country. Bull Connor's methods were compared with the "unleashing of Communist soldiers against peaceful demonstrators in Eastern Europe." "The conscience and sense of justice of the American people should be shaken by Birmingham," said one Kentucky senator.

Birmingham was ready to give up. Just as the surging force of the fire hoses had thrown the demonstrators to their knees, so now the surging force of thousands of black people had brought Birmingham to its knees. Business was being ruined. The city was on the verge of widespread rioting. Two thousand black people filled the jails, and more stood ready to go to jail. White business leaders were ready to sit down and talk. "Call a truce," they said. "What are your demands?" For two days the negotiating went on. Then a four-point settlement was announced. It called for:

1. The desegregation of lunch counters, rest rooms, fitting rooms, and drinking fountains in all downtown stores within ninety days.

2. The placement of Negroes in previously all-white clerical and sales positions in the stores through promotion or hiring within sixty days.

3. Release of prisoners.

4. The establishment of a biracial committee to permit permanent communication between white and black leaders.

As he announced the settlement, King urged his people to "move from protest to reconciliation."

The business community may have made its peace with the demonstrators, but others had not. That night, the peace of the settlement was broken by two bombings. A.D. King's home and the Gaston Motel were bombed. The bombings spurred mobs of black people (most of them not part of the nonviolent movement) to go on a rioting and looting rampage. SCLC, police, firefighters, and Civil Defense workers managed to restore peace after three hours.

The next day efforts were made to keep the peace. Army units and the Alabama National Guard were put on standby. King and Abernathy went on a walking tour of the pool halls, restaurants, bars, and shops urging people not to beat up any police officers or burn down any stores. Then the people were led in a chorus of "We Shall Overcome."

A week later, on May 20, the Supreme Court declared Birmingham's segregation laws unconstitutional.

In June, President John F. Kennedy announced to the nation that he was requesting Congress to act at once on the most comprehensive civil rights bill so far.

"We preach freedom around the world," said the president, "and we cherish our freedom here at home, but are we here to say to the world . . . that this is a land of the free, except for the Negroes? . . . Now the time has come for this nation to fulfill its promise. The events in Birmingham and elsewhere have so increased the cries for equality, that no city or state can ignore them." They were strong words coming from a president. Just the words that King had been saying for many years. But no president had ever said them.

In September, when Birmingham had settled down, the diehards fired one last vicious shot. They bombed the Sixteenth Street Baptist Church, which had been the assembly center for the children's marches. The bomb was thrown through the window of a Sunday school classroom. Four little girls were killed and twenty-one were injured.

Preaching at the funeral of the girls, King said, "Their death says to us that we must work unceasingly to make the American dream a reality. . . . The innocent blood of these little girls may well serve as the redemptive force that will bring new light to this dark city."

Gradually new light did come to Birmingham. Perhaps a Birmingham business leader saw the first glimmers of light. "Am I just imagining it," he asked, "or are the Negroes around town walking a little straighter these days?"

Black Birmingham had found its pride. Things would get better for them in their hometown.

"I HAVE A DREAM!"

5

The victory in Birmingham was followed by dozens of similar campaigns. In Jackson, Mississippi, in Rome, Georgia, in Danville, Virginia, and in Cambridge, Maryland, black people marched, sat in, and boycotted. During the ten weeks following Birmingham, there were 758 demonstrations in 186 cities. And there were growing numbers of white faces seen in the marches and demonstrations. These white people really could not grasp the pain and frustration of being black, but they were "sickened and disgusted" by some of the events in Birmingham, and they wanted to do their part. Black hopes were growing, and things were not happening fast enough to satisfy those hopes.

In the northern cities, blacks weren't worried about "colored only" signs or separate drinking fountains. For them the problem was jobs. Discrimination forced them to take low-paying menial jobs or live on welfare. This was the kind of defeat they lived with every day. So when King visited Harlem, they threw eggs at him.

It was clear to King that the movement was no longer a southern movement. It had become a national effort and now it was time to focus on the problems of black people in the North. The civil rights bill proposed to Congress by the president was a first step. Soon Congress would be considering the bill. What was needed was a way to show Congress that the American people, black *and* white, wanted this bill passed. King met with other civil rights leaders to discuss this goal. A. Philip Randolph suggested a march on Washington. Congress could hardly ignore thousands of people marching from the Washington Monument to the Lincoln Memorial. King and the others agreed that a march was a good idea. So planning for the March on Washington for Jobs and Freedom began.

More than two hundred people—including union officials, leaders of Protestant, Catholic, and Jewish organizations, and civil rights leaders—formed a march committee. At a July 2 meeting in New York City, they discussed recruiting the members of their organization to march and made plans to raise money to pay the expenses for the march.

Bayard Rustin, who had worked for King in SCLC for several years, was appointed deputy director of the march. His job was to make all the preparations. The marchers would need drinking water, food, and first-aid stations. Rustin recruited speakers, entertainers, bands, and congressmen to join the march. He planned the schedule for the day.

Every precaution was taken to keep order during the march. Two thousand black New York City police officers volunteered to serve as marshals. More than eight thousand police officers, National Guard troops, and other troops would be on standby. Wrote Rustin in a letter to the march committee, "We are asking each person to be a marshal of himself, since anybody who turns to violence will be a traitor to our cause."

By bus, by train, by plane, by car—the people came to Washington on August 28, 1963, to march for jobs and freedom. They began gathering near the Washington Monument just after midnight. By 10 A.M. there were forty thousand people clustered near the monument. And just an hour later the number had more than doubled. The march was sched-

Two hundred thousand strong came to the March on Washington for Jobs and Freedom on August 28, 1963.

uled to begin at 11:30, but a Washington high school drum and bugle corps started off at 11:20 and everyone else followed, leaving the civil rights leaders behind. "My God," said one leader, "they're going! We're supposed to be leading them."

King smiled and said to the person marching beside him, "A revolution is supposed to be unpredictable."

The long procession of people, black and white, slowly made its way to the Lincoln Memorial. They sang, many joined hands, and some waved banners reading "Freedom Now!" As they marched, fathers hoisted toddlers to their shoulders, old people held onto each other, and ties and jackets came off beneath the noon sun. By 1 P.M., more than two hundred thousand people—a third of them white—stood before the Lincoln Memorial. Gathered on the platform in the shadow of the Great Emancipator were movie stars such as Sidney Poitier and Marlon Brando, singers Lena Horne and Sammy Davis, Jr., baseball player Jackie Robinson, diplomat Ralph Bunche, and 150 members of Congress. Black singer Camilla Williams opened the rally with the "Star Spangled Banner." Then came the speeches.

"We came here because we love our country," said Rev. Fred Shuttlesworth. This Birmingham civil rights leader had marched beside King in Birmingham. "Our country needs us and we need our country. Everybody in America ought to be free. If the politicians want peace, if the judges want to unclog their court calendars, then turn the Negro loose in America! Then we'll all be free."

In his deep, booming voice, A. Philip Randolph spoke to the crowd. "We are the advance guard of a massive moral revolution for jobs and freedom. This revolution reverberates throughout the land, touching every city, every town, every village where black men are segregated, oppressed and exploited. . . ."

Then came more singing. Bob Dylan sang about the shooting of civil rights worker Medgar Evers. Odetta sang about freedom. Joan Baez sang "We Shall Overcome." There were speeches by white ministers and rabbis. John

Lewis, president of SNCC spoke. This man had been beaten twelve times and arrested twenty-two times. His speech was angry and demanding. "Listen, Mr. Kennedy, listen, Mr. Congressman, listen, fellow citizens—the black masses are on the march for jobs and freedom, and there won't be a cooling off period. We want our freedom, and we want it now!"

It was a hot day, and some marchers who were drifting away changed their minds when gospel singer Mahalia Jackson took her turn before the microphone. She soon had the entire assembly clapping to her singing of "I Been 'Buked and I Been Scorned."

The next speaker was Martin Luther King, Jr. As he approached the microphone, the crowd began to chant and cheer and wave their banners. It was more than a minute before the uproar subsided. As King began to speak, a hush came over the crowd. He spoke of the debt America owed to its black citizens, of freedom not yet fulfilled.

"I have a dream," he said, "a dream deeply rooted in the American dream. I have a dream that one day this nation will rise up and live out the true meaning of its creed: 'We hold these truths to be self-evident, that all men are created equal.'

"I have a dream that one day on the red hills of Georgia, the sons of former slaves and the sons of former slave-owners will be able to sit together at the table of brotherhood.

"I have a dream that one day even the state of Mississippi will be transformed into an oasis of freedom and justice.

"I have a dream that my four little children will one day live in a nation where they will not be judged by the color of their skin, but by the content of their character.

"And if America is to be a great nation, this must become true. So let freedom ring."

King ended with the hope that someday all Americans could join hands and sing the words of an old Negro spiritual, "Free at last! Free at last! Thank God almighty, we are free at last!"

As King finished, the people cheered and clapped; some

King delivers his famous "I have a dream" speech at the Lincoln Memorial.

were in tears. As the marchers turned to go, many were quiet, thinking about the day's events. It was an historic occasion, the largest such rally ever, and they had been a part of it. Many left Washington that day with a firm resolve to go home and keep working for the "dream" and the "freedom at last" that King had mentioned.

But members of Congress were not impressed by the great gathering in Washington. Senator Hubert Humphrey, who was a firm backer of the civil rights bill up for consideration, doubted that the march would change any votes. "But it's a good thing for Washington and the nation and the world," he said.

After the march, the civil rights leaders met with President Kennedy. They discussed the goals of the march and whether the proposed civil rights bill would bring them about. These goals covered all the problems blacks had encountered in America, from segregated housing and schools, to lack of job opportunity and job training, to protection of voting rights. The president said he doubted that all the goals would be guaranteed by the new bill. He believed that the march may have influenced some votes, but that King and the others must continue to lobby for the bill.

A few months later, President Kennedy was assassinated. And now there was a southerner in the White House. King was happily impressed by Lyndon Johnson's assurance that he would continue to push for civil rights as Kennedy had. Johnson would prove to be an even more courageous friend of black people than Kennedy. And Johnson, who had served in Congress for many years, wielded a great deal of influence among the lawmakers. He was able to gather much support for bills he favored.

Shortly after he came into office, Johnson announced his War on Poverty. This program was intended to alleviate the problems that caused poverty, in particular, poor education and lack of jobs.

In the spring of 1964, King joined another campaign for civil rights begun in St. Augustine, Florida. He had become increasingly concerned about the violence sweeping the country. It was this climate of violence which inspired the assassination of Kennedy. Violence against Negroes was particularly bad in St. Augustine, a totally segregated city. Segregationists attacked black demonstrators with chains, clubs, and even containers of acid. For the most part, the police did little to stop the violence.

King brought his nonviolent campaign to St. Augustine. He was certain that beneath the brutality of every segregationist was a conscience. But his first rally produced no evidence of this. As the demonstrators knelt to pray, a member of the white segregationist Ku Klux Klan shouted, "Niggers ain't got no God!" and moved in to club one of the kneelers. It was a cruel and vicious act. But what was worse, the police simply stood and watched, making no arrests.

In the days to come, the scene was basically the same— brutal mobs and police looking the other way. Finally, Governor Farris Bryant sent in state troopers to protect the demonstrators. Most of the mob violence ended.

King tried to have dinner at a segregated restaurant. "We can't serve you here," said the owner. "We will stand here," said King. The owner said that King could eat in the kitchen. "Do you understand what this does to our dignity?" asked King. The owner called the police and had King arrested. After two days King was released on bail.

Violence returned to the city. Blacks and whites had armed themselves and were shooting into homes and cars. A group of blacks and whites jumped into a "whites only" swimming pool. The owner poured acid into the water. When this didn't force the demonstrators out of the pool, the owner called the police and had the demonstrators arrested. Wade-ins were held at segregated beaches. State troopers had to be called in to protect the demonstrators from the angry mobs.

Finally, the business leaders of St. Augustine agreed to desegregate their businesses. But they were pressured by segregationists to back out of the agreement. Not until the

Civil Rights Act of 1964 was signed by President Johnson on July 2 did St. Augustine desegregate. Said the president on signing the bill, "This new law does not give special treatment to any citizen. It does, however, say that those who are equal before God shall now also be equal in the polling booths, in the classrooms, in the factories, and in hotels and restaurants and movie theaters and other places that provide service to the public." What the 1954 bill had *implied* by outlawing segregation in the schools, this bill flatly said: "No more segregation in public places." The bill, sometimes called the Public Accommodations Act, also prohibited employers or unions from discriminating against blacks in hiring. The act created the Equal Employment Opportunity Commission.

It was a long, hot summer in the North. And the black neighborhoods in Jersey City, Philadelphia, Rochester, and New York City's Harlem exploded in rioting, born of the frustration of unfulfilled hopes. It was clear to King that the Civil Rights Act hadn't done much for the rioters.

In October 1964 King was notified that he had been selected as the 1964 Nobel Peace Prize winner. The honor bestowed on King was an international recognition of the American Negro's struggle for full equality in American society.

King and his family traveled to Oslo, Norway, in December to receive the award. The presentation was held at Oslo University auditorium. Dr. Gunnar Jahn, chairman of the Nobel Committee, introduced King as "an undaunted champion of peace . . . first person in the Western world to have shown us that a struggle can be waged without violence."

Then King began to speak. "I conclude that this award is a profound recognition that nonviolence is the answer to the crucial political and moral question of our time—the need for man to overcome oppression and violence. . . . The tortuous road which has led from Montgomery, Alabama, to Oslo bears witness to this truth."

When he returned to Atlanta, the city held a banquet in his honor. The little boy who couldn't sit in the front of a downtown shoe store had grown up and was the honored guest at a downtown hotel. Blacks and whites joined hands and sang "We Shall Overcome." All around him was evidence that what he was trying to do was working. But he didn't intend to stop. As he told the banquet guests at the end of his speech, "I must return to the valley all over the South and in the big cities of the North—a valley filled with millions of our white and Negro brothers who are smothering in an airtight cage of poverty in the midst of an affluent society."

"MARCHING FOR THE VOTE"

6

In January 1965 King went "back to the valley," to Selma, Alabama—a valley of despair for black people. It was a valley yet untouched by desegregation. The city of Selma had had a particularly bitter post–Civil War experience. It had been almost completely destroyed by Union forces and had later been occupied by a black regiment. Selma had not forgotten or forgiven. White people of Selma expressed this bitterness in their cruel and unjust treatment of black people. Some white people had very "educated" ways of explaining the terrible racial oppression for which Selma was known. "You see," said a judge, "most of your Selma Negroes are descended from Ibo and Angola tribes of Africa. You could never teach or trust Ibo back in slave days, and even today I can spot their tribal characteristics. They have protruding heels, for instance."

In addition to its rigid segregation, Selma had a most amazing voter registration record. Of the twenty-nine thousand people in Selma, more than half were black, yet only 350 blacks were registered to vote.

At a rally on January 2, 1965, held in Selma's Browns Chapel A.M.E. Church, King announced an assault on Selma's voter registration record. "We will march on the ballot boxes by the thousands. . . . We must be willing to go to jail by the thousands. We are not asking, we are demanding the ballot."

Selma's reputation had been seriously damaged by racial conflict the year before. Its new mayor was determined to avoid further violence, because the city was in the midst of a campaign to lure northern industry to its area. He knew that one news picture could turn national opinion against Selma. So Selma's official policy toward the upcoming King campaign would be to meet nonviolence with nonviolence.

Thus it was that police stood by quietly as King checked into Selma's Hotel Albert. It was the first time a black person had ever signed the hotel register. The sight of King standing at the registration desk was too much for one young white man. He rushed up to King and began to beat him with his fists. The man was quickly arrested by police. "We're simply trying to enforce the law in an impartial manner," said the police captain.

Captain J. Wilson Baker had just been hired by the city. This professional law enforcer did not believe in police brutality and did not encourage or condone the cruel treatment of black people by police. One of his missions was to undercut County Sheriff Jim Clark, who was in many ways Selma's Bull Connor. Sheriff Clark had been keeping "blacks in their place" for years and saw no reason to change now.

The voter registration campaign in Selma began with small groups of twenty black people marching to the county courthouse to register to vote. Sheriff Clark, as a county law officer, was assigned to keep order at the scene. As black people approached the courthouse, Clark would not let them enter or wait near the front door. He ordered them to form a line in a side alley. Those who refused to obey his order were arrested. One black woman who was leading a group was roughly dragged off to a police car by Clark. Time and time again, as black people gathered near the front door of the courthouse, they were arrested. "You are here to cause trouble," Clark said to the blacks. "If you do not disperse you will be under arrest."

Captain Baker tried to convince Clark to stop these arrests, but Clark refused. Then one day Baker appeared on the scene. He told the black people approaching the courthouse that they could wait near the front door of the courthouse if they formed an orderly line. This they did as an unbelieving Clark looked on. Clark walked to the front of the line and shouted, "You have one minute to leave this area." The one hundred black people forming the line didn't move. Clark arrested them.

Because of the arrests, the black voters' registration was proceeding very slowly. King decided to lead a group of 260 demonstrators to the courthouse. Such an action would be in direct violation of Selma's law, which required that any group of more than twenty people walking together had to have a parade permit. The group met at Browns Chapel on February 1 and set out through the cold drizzle. They had walked less than three blocks when they found their way barred by Baker. "This is a deliberate attempt to violate the law," said Baker. "You will have to break up into small groups."

"We feel that we have a constitutional right to walk down to the courthouse," said King.

King and the others were arrested. On that same day several hundred schoolchildren picketing the courthouse were arrested. The arrests made the headlines. Selma was labeled as the city that had jailed a Nobel Prize winner. King was released on bail a few days later.

More marches took place. The marchers were politely arrested. A Lutheran minister from nearby Birmingham led an all-white demonstration; those marchers were arrested, too. Then, gradually, Selma faded from the headlines, and the country lost interest in the Selma campaign.

On February 18, Jimmie Lee Jackson, a black man, was shot while taking part in a demonstration in nearby Marion, Alabama. The marchers had been attacked by a white mob and state troopers. Jackson, who lived for ten days after the shooting, said he had been shot by a trooper.

King, speaking at Jackson's funeral, pledged to "work unrelentingly to make the American dream a reality."

King began to plan a march from Selma to the state capital of Montgomery, to protest Jackson's death. Alabama Governor George Wallace issued a ban against the march and ordered the state troopers to do whatever was necessary to stop the marchers. But plans for the march continued.

On Sunday, March 7, more than five hundred people gathered at Browns Chapel to make the 54-mile (86-km) march. They came prepared with food and blankets.

Two by two, the marchers stepped out. After walking six blocks, they came to the Edmund Pettus Bridge. Once across the bridge, the marchers would be on Highway 80 and on their way to Montgomery. As they approached the bridge, the marchers could see a line of state troopers blocking the far side of the bridge. They started across the bridge. The troopers donned gas masks and raised their nightsticks over their heads.

"Halt!" said the major in command of the troopers.

The marchers did so.

"This is an unlawful assembly . . . not conducive to public safety," said the major. "Go back to your church or to your homes."

"May we have a word with the major?" replied Hosea Williams, SCLC leader of the march.

"There is no word to be had," was the reply. "You have two minutes to turn around and go back to your church."

The marchers stood their ground.

"Troopers, advance!" came the order.

Hurling tear gas canisters and swinging their nightsticks, the troopers charged the marchers. A gray cloud of tear gas smoke covered the area. The troopers clubbed the marchers in the front part of the line. At once the scene became one of bleeding, coughing marchers and troopers lashing out with their nightsticks.

Across the street a group of white onlookers cheered and gave the screeching rebel yell, a yell Confederate troops had given when they went into battle during the Civil War.

"Please, no! God, we're being killed!" screamed one black woman.

At this point some of the marchers began to throw stones at the troopers. Others fell to their knees in prayer. Many began to run.

The troopers, joined by Sheriff Clark and a volunteer posse, drove all the marchers back to the Browns Chapel church. At the church an all-out battle of rocks, bottles, and nightsticks began. Then Baker stepped in. He urged the marchers to go into the church and ordered the troopers and posse to cease their attack.

Fifty marchers were hurt that day, with sixteen requiring hospitalization for treatment of fractured skulls and broken ribs.

Again Selma was in the news. "Bloody Sunday," it was called. Pictures of unarmed marchers being beaten by troopers inspired national sympathy and concern for the voters' crusade taking place in Selma.

On Monday, King again called for a march from Selma to Montgomery. He urged American clergy to come to Selma to join the march. The response was remarkable; four hundred rabbis, ministers, and priests arrived in Selma to march.

In the meantime, the federal court had banned the march, and President Johnson made a special request that the ban be obeyed. King was being urged by some of his followers to ignore the ban. He had felt it necessary to remain in Atlanta on Bloody Sunday in order to tend to some church business. He had been accused of "chickening out" of the Bloody Sunday march. Now, King wanted to march very much. He knew that his followers were ready to go and their enthusiasm and dedication might evaporate if they didn't march.

But black people had a good friend in the White House. King did not want to antagonize such a powerful friend. Still, the injunction that banned the march was unjust, and King believed that a person could violate unjust laws and court orders. Finally, King agreed to a compromise suggested by Florida Governor LeRoy Collins. The idea was that the demonstrators march to the bridge, kneel and pray, and then retrace their steps. They could have their march, but as long as they did not leave the Selma city limits they would not be in violation of the ban.

On Tuesday, fifteen hundred marchers led by King walked to the bridge, knelt, and, led by the clergy, prayed for fifteen minutes. Then they returned to the church.

There had been no violence. The country and Selma breathed easier. But not for long.

That night three white ministers who had come to Selma to march ate dinner in a black restaurant. As they left they were attacked by a group of whites. Rev. James J. Reeb, a Unitarian minister from Boston, was struck in the back of the head with a large club wielded by one of the attackers. Rev. Reeb dropped to the ground like a rock. The minister was taken to the hospital, and white and black demonstrators turned out in the streets to pray for him. Even when a chilling rain began to fall, they kept their vigil. But Reeb died two days after he was attacked.

Reeb's death touched off a wave of sympathy for the black-voting-rights cause. In cities across the country, tens of thousands of white and black people marched through the streets, demanding federal intervention in Selma. The White House was picketed by white clergy, black militants, and students.

A few days later, President Johnson addressed a joint session of Congress. The presidential message included words that King had never dreamed he would hear from the White House. They were things he had thought about in college and many times since Montgomery. Truly this president understood the meaning of the black cause.

In part, the president's words were:

What happened in Selma is part of a far larger movement which reaches into every section and state of America. It is the effort of American Negroes to secure for themselves the full blessings of American life.

Their cause must be our cause, too. Because it's not just Negroes, but really all of us, who must overcome the crippling legacy of bigotry and injustice.

We shall overcome.

The real hero of this struggle is the American Negro. His actions and protests, his courage to risk safety, and even to risk his life, have awakened the conscience of this nation. His demonstrations have been designed to call attention to injustice; designed to provoke change; designed to stir reform.

He has called upon us to make good the promise of America. And who among us can say that we would have made the same progress were it not for his persistent bravery and his faith in American democracy.

The president then promised to write a bill that would firmly guarantee the voting rights of all Americans. He urged Congress to give the bill top priority.

King was pleased to see that the struggle in Selma had brought the whole issue of the right to vote to the forefront of the nation's priorities. But he did not intend to call a halt to the demonstrations. "We must keep the issue alive and the urgency of it before the nation," he told a news reporter.

Six hundred marchers demonstrated at the Montgomery courthouse that very afternoon. And again there was violence and injury when the demonstrators were attacked by troopers and Sheriff Clark's posse. Eight people were hurt, and the demonstrators were angrily planning "to tie up every street and bus and commit every act of civil disobedience ever seen." King managed to calm their anger and promised to lead them in a peaceful march the next day.

The following morning as a gentle rain fell, fifteen hundred marchers set out to walk to the courthouse. They were guarded by a police escort and reached the courthouse with no problems. Speaking through a megaphone from the steps of the courthouse, King gave the demonstrators some good news. A federal judge had just ruled that they could make their Selma-to-Montgomery march. The demonstrators cheered.

The plan for the five-day march approved by the judge called for no more than three hundred people to make the full march. The marchers would sleep in tents pitched along the road at night. In order to protect the marchers as they went, the president ordered the Alabama National Guard and army units to stand by.

"It is my prayer," said the president in a message to the nation, "that the march . . . may proceed in a manner honoring our heritage and . . . all for which America stands."

Thousands of Americans, black and white, the famous and the not so famous, poured into Selma to take part in the march set for March 21. On that day thirty-two hundred people gathered at the Browns Chapel church. Standing on the steps of the church, King spoke to the marchers. "Walk together, children; don't you get weary, and it will lead us to the Promised Land. And Alabama will be a new Alabama and America will be a new America." The march began. Arms linked, the marchers sang their anthem, "We Shall Overcome." An army escort marched alongside to protect them. Overhead helicopters watched for snipers. Bomb experts watched for booby traps.

Among those who had come to watch the marchers leave was Sheriff Clark. He wore a large button on his coat which read "NEVER," his answer to black cries for "Freedom Now." Other white onlookers held up hastily scrawled signs which read "Nigger Lover," "Bye, Bye, Blackbird," and "Martin Luther Coon."

The marchers crossed the Pettus Bridge and headed down Highway 80 toward Montgomery. They marched a little more than 7 miles (11 km) and then made camp for the night. Three hundred continued, and the rest returned by bus to Selma. Along the way the marchers had to endure more insults."Yankee trash, go home," "Filthy scum . . . sewer rats." But they also encountered some friendly people. One elderly black man hobbled along with them for a mile (1.6

*An impromptu news conference with King
as he leads civil rights demonstrators
in a march to Montgomery.*

km). Then, waving his cane at them, he said goodbye. "I just wanted to walk one mile with y'all," he said. "I been called 'boy' long enough, don't you think?"

By Wednesday afternoon the marchers had reached the outskirts of Montgomery. Others came to join the march. That night they camped on a large athletic field near the city. Entertainers such as Harry Belafonte, Leonard Bernstein, Tony Bennet, Sammy Davis, Jr., Ruby Dee, Bobby Darin, Shelly Winters, and many more gave a show for the tired marchers.

The next day more people joined the march. By afternoon, twenty-five thousand people had moved through Montgomery's streets toward the state capitol. As they stood outside the capitol, Governor Wallace watched them through his venetian blinds. He saw twenty-five thousand people, black and white, from all over America who believed that blacks should have the right to vote in Selma.

"That's quite a crowd," the governor was heard to say. He refused to meet with the leaders of the march to listen to their demands.

Now it was time for the speeches. It had been ten years since the Montgomery bus boycott, and much had been accomplished. Said King, "I stand before you this afternoon with the conviction that segregation is on its deathbed in Alabama. I know some of you are asking 'How long will it take?' I come to say to you this afternoon, however difficult the moment, however frustrating the hour, it will not be long because truth pressed to earth will rise again. How long? Not long, because no lie can live forever. . . ."

The marchers knew that victory was near. The governor may have turned a deaf ear to their demands, but the country was behind them.

As the speeches ended, the tired marchers returned to their homes, content in the knowledge that they had made it from Selma to Montgomery and that no violence had marred their pilgrimage.

Volunteer drivers transported the marchers back to Selma. Viola Liuzzo, a white volunteer driver from Detroit, had taken some marchers to Selma and was returning for others.

A car pulled up alongside hers and she was shot to death. Once again, the murderous violence of a few whites had marred the peace-making efforts of many whites. SCLC and the nation went into mourning, vowing that spilled blood would make them work harder to reach their goal.

The Federal Bureau of Investigation began a determined search for the killers. Within a day, four men, all members of the Ku Klux Klan, were arrested and charged with murder. The president announced an all-out federal attack on the KKK. He called them "the enemies of justice, who for decades have used the rope and the gun, the tar and the feathers to terrorize their neighbors." The president promised laws that would make it impossible for the Klan to survive.

During the summer Selma's voting registrars continued to drag their feet, and the governor continued to look the other way. Then, on August 6, 1965, the president signed the Voting Rights Bill into law. A White House official had told reporters that the bill would work automatically. "If a state won't register an American citizen, then the Federal Government will. We'll get them registered, and we'll get them voted, too."

Within ten days after the bill was signed, twenty thousand black people had registered to vote for the first time. They had "walked together" and, just as King had said, they were drawing near to the "promised land."

Even as the black voter registration continued, King was setting his sights on a new goal. Black people needed good jobs.

CHALLENGE IN THE NORTH, DEATH IN THE SOUTH

7

Watts lies south of the exclusive shops of downtown Los Angeles and the swimming pools of Beverly Hills. It is far from the sea breezes of fancy beach communities like Redondo Beach. Sandwiched between two major expressways, Watts was home for more than eighty thousand black people in 1965. Cut off from the city by the lack of good public transportation, cut off from the good life outside by lack of good paying jobs and housing discrimination, the residents of Watts tried to make the best of their tumbledown neighborhood. Magnificent Montague, a disc jockey, helped them get through the day. He could be picked up on station KGFJ from 7 A.M. until 10 P.M.. In between the rhythm-and-blues records, he provided the usual disc jockey chatter. One of his favorite expressions was "Burn, baby, burn." No one knew what it meant. But it sounded cool. Teenagers loved to imitate it. It quickly became one of the "in" expressions of Watts.

Then one hot Wednesday night in August, Watts found good use for their "in" expression. Watts was a tinderbox of bitterness and despair that hot night. It required only a spark to ignite it. That spark was the routine arrest of a black man for driving while drunk. As a crowd gathered to watch the proceedings, the police became frightened. In their haste to arrest the driver and leave, they manhandled him. His brother and mother, rushing to his defense, were also arrested. The watching crowd grew angrier.

As the police sped away with their three prisoners, the message that went out over squad car radios was "Police cars—stay out of Watts. Repeat, Remain out of Watts." It was hoped that without the antagonizing sight of police, the dangerously developing situation might simmer down.

After a few hours police patrols were sent back into Watts to survey the situation. Groups of angry blacks swarmed through the streets. They threw bottles at the police, and a police sergeant ordered a retreat. False rumors fueled the anger of the mobs. "The cops beat a pregnant girl to death. Saw it myself." "Cops took a boy out of a car, pushed him against a wall, and busted his head wide open."

An elderly white couple traveling through Watts in their car were set upon by a large group of black teenagers who climbed on the car, opened the doors, dragged the two people out, and beat them. Then they set the car on fire. One teenager stood on top of a car parked nearby and, stretching his arms out, chanted "Burn, baby, burn!" Thus the riot started. For four days, the looting and the burning went on. Drivers who ventured into Watts emerged with bleeding faces and battered vehicles. By day the looters and arsonists rested, waiting until night to come out and resume the riot.

The police did not seem to have a plan and did not ask for help from the state highway patrol. Not until Friday, two days later, did the governor's office order the National Guard into Watts. Still the rioting went on. More troops were ordered in. By Sunday, when the riot finally ended, thirteen thousand troops and one thousand police were patrolling the area.

It was the bloodiest, most destructive race riot in American history. When it was over, thirty-six people were dead, more than a thousand had been hurt, nearly four thousand were in jail, and forty million dollars' worth of property had been looted, burned, or wrecked.

What bigotry and repression had not done to Watts, Watts had done to itself during those terrible August days. There was no place to buy food or medicine. Many homes were without electricity.

King was attending a meeting in Puerto Rico when he heard the news of the riot. He knew nothing about Watts and had no SCLC offices or friends in the area. But he felt it was his duty to rush to the troubled area. He immediately got on a plane for Los Angeles. It was his intention to drive through the streets, tell people who he was, and urge them to be nonviolent.

King arrived in Watts on Sunday. Fires were still smouldering. It had been arranged for him to speak at the dilapidated office of a community organization. Five hundred people crowded into the small room to hear him. King quickly found out that he had more to learn from the crowd than they from him.

"The people don't feel bad about what happened," said one man. "They have nothing to lose. They don't have jobs, decent homes. What else could they do?"

"Burn, baby, burn!" yelled one teenager.

"All over America," said King, "the Negroes must join hands—"

"And burn, baby, burn," said one man standing in the door.

"—and work together in a creative way," said King.

"The mayor and the chief of police should come down here and see how we're living," said one woman.

"And they would burn the most," said a teenage girl.

King promised to get Mayor Yorty and Chief Parker to come to Watts.

"You'll have to drag them," shouted one woman.

Finally, King managed to give a small talk. "I'm here," he said, "because at the bottom we are brothers and sisters,

*King talks with a group
of Watts residents.*

and whatever pains you pains me. When you suffer, I suffer. We are not free in the South and you are not free in the cities of the North." He said he knew that they had legitimate complaints, but he begged them not to hate white people.

"There will be a better tomorrow," he said.

"When, dammit, when?" asked an insistent teenage boy wearing a tattered shirt.

"We shall overcome," said King.

He left the meeting with the bitter words of people in distress filling his thoughts. Once on the street, he stopped to talk to a group of small boys.

"We won," said one of the boys.

"How can you say you won," asked King, "when thirty-four black people are dead, your community is in ruins, and whites are using the riot as an excuse to do nothing?"

"We won because we made them pay attention to us," was the answer.

It was true, King realized. No one had paid attention to Watts until the riot. King had never even heard of Watts until the riot. Now here he was, visiting Watts and wanting to help. But he could offer no satisfactory response to "Burn, baby, burn!"

Later King met with the mayor and the chief of police, who felt that law and order would solve the problems. "Law and order cannot be authentic unless you have justice and human dignity in a community," King pointed out to the officials. While they listened politely, they did not understand.

These officials had no idea what it was like to live in Watts and how lack of jobs and good housing robbed people of their dignity. Unemployment in Watts compared with that during the height of the Great Depression. An acute housing shortage forced two and three families to crowd into one apartment. And California had just repealed its law against housing discrimination. The residents of the Watts ghetto felt trapped. To make matters worse, television brought them images of the better life, a life which, it seemed, would never be theirs. There is probably no one more dangerous or unpredictable than a person without hope.

King was asked to write an article about Watts for the magazine *Saturday Review.* In the article he wrote of his efforts to help the black person in the South. He had believed that achieving his goals of desegregation and voting rights in the South would cause the nation to search its conscience and so provide all black Americans with their rights. But this had not happened. Instead, as nonviolence improved conditions in the South, conditions in the black slums of the North got worse. Dilapidated homes became older. Segregation in schools increased. Northern blacks experienced little of the prospering economy; for them unemployment rose. While the country shuddered at the brutality of fire hoses and dogs in Birmingham, police brutality in the North continued to be ignored.

As a high school student King had been delighted by the free society he had found in the North. Now he realized that just beneath the freedom he thought he had seen in the North lay cruel economic realities which forced generation upon generation to live on public assistance. King had not really seen the housing conditions which were, in many ways, far worse than anything the southern black person had to endure.

It was time, wrote King, to focus the black freedom movement on conditions in the North. The question was: Would black demands for justice in the North be violent or nonviolent? Northern white leadership could no longer rely on small changes and substitutes to satisfy those demands. It is clear, he wrote, that black communities in the North had run out of patience and intended to put an end to the long train of abuses they had endured. In Watts people had resorted to violence in desperation, and they had succeeded in getting attention. But nonviolence would have gotten just as much attention, and Watts would not now be in ruins, he wrote.

As he considered the new goals of better jobs and better housing for black people, King realized that the white population would probably resist stubbornly. The reason was money. Allowing a black person to vote or sit at a lunch counter or register in a hotel didn't cost money. But giving the black person an equal chance for a job could deprive a white person of that job. Better housing and better schools for black people could raise taxes.

King remembered something Hyman Bookbinder, assistant director of the Office of Economic Opportunity, had said. "The long-range cost of . . . programs to fight poverty, ignorance and slums will reach one trillion dollars. . . . The poor can stop being poor if the rich are willing to become even richer at a slower rate. . . . Unless a substantial sacrifice is made by the American people, the nation can expect further deterioration of the cities, increased antagonisms between races and continued disorders in the streets."

It was clear that reaching the goal would be difficult. But the patience of black people in the cities was wearing thin. Something had to be done quickly to avoid more violence. King was not certain that nonviolence would work in the North, but he decided to try; the alternative was too horrible to think about.

King selected Chicago as his target northern city. Here he would test nonviolence. The goals would be better housing, better jobs, and better schools. Of Chicago's three and a half million population, one million were black people. One in four employable black people did not have a job. In one large 50-square-mile (130-sq-km) black neighborhood, nearly half the housing was dilapidated, and many buildings lacked adequate plumbing. The city spent an average of $266 per year to educate a black child compared with $366 per year to educate a white child.

In January 1966 King and his wife moved into a slum apartment in the Lawndale section of Chicago. SCLC staff members had begun visiting people and holding meetings to recruit people to take part in protests. "I have never seen such hopelessness," said one SCLC staffer. "The Negroes of Chicago have a greater feeling of powerlessness than any I ever saw. We're used to working with people who want to be freed. The Chicago Negro is beaten down psychologically."

Thus SCLC's first task was to find ways to revive the withered hopes of Chicago's black slum dwellers. In the South people's hopes were kept alive by religion, but most residents of Chicago's black ghetto did not have close ties to religion. Among these bitter and despairing people King saw little evidence of the togetherness or community that also keeps hope alive. Two community organizations were set up, the Union to End Slums and the Community Renewal Society. The guiding theme of these organizations was "You've got to hit those cats where it hurts most—in the pocketbook." Working through these organizations a dozen tenant unions forced landlords to repair their buildings by withholding rent. Boycotts of businesses in ghetto neighborhoods forced merchants to hire black people. This tactic also persuaded merchants to sell products made by black manufacturers and to bank at black banks.

Working together and getting results helped the people to hope again. King often spurred them on with one of his stirring speeches at rallies.

"We are victims of slumism! Listen, we must straighten up our backs!

"What is our problem?

"It is that we are powerless. How do we get power?

"By organizing ourselves. By getting together.

"We are somebody because we are God's children.

"You don't need to hate anybody. You don't need any Molotov cocktails [gasoline bombs]. A riot can always be stopped by superior force. But they can't stop thousands of feet marching nonviolently.

"We're going to change the whole Jericho road!"

As one, the people were on their feet, clapping and cheering. It was good to think that you could organize and do something—that you were somebody.

King with his wife, Coretta, shortly after they moved into a Chicago slum neighborhood.

The small rallies were only rehearsals for a large rally planned for July 10 in Chicago's Soldier's Field. Once the rally had gotten the city's attention, King intended to meet with the mayor and present demands for better jobs and housing for black people.

Even as King worked to restore the hope of Chicago's black ghetto, a new rallying cry was rising from some black leaders. That cry was "black power." It was a controversial battle cry which threatened to split the civil rights movement down the middle. To King, "black power" meant that the black person did not want to be a part of America, but separate. King had always worked toward the goal of black and white together. "Black power" meant abandoning that hope.

SNCC president Stokely Carmichael insisted that "black power" meant economic and political power. King pointed out that black people could not get that kind of power without the help of white people. "Why not use the words 'black equality' or 'black consciousness'?" he asked. " 'Black power' sounds better," was the answer. To King, "black power" was the bitter cry of surrender. It said to white America, "I don't care that you won't let me be a full-fledged citizen of this country. I'll get 'black power.' " "Black power," the cry of those without hope, was often heard in Chicago those days.

The mass rally at Soldier's Field drew a crowd of forty-five thousand people. Speaking to the crowd, King said, "Our power is in our unity." He urged the people to avoid the violence, because it would not achieve their goal. He said that their power was in their marching feet, not in bricks and knives. In the crowd he could see gangs of teenagers waving banners reading "Black Power."

After the speeches, King led a march to city hall. There he attached a list of demands to the door of city hall. Housing, education, jobs, and a just and open city were the demands. The next day Mayor Richard Daley met with King to discuss the demands. Daley told King that he supported civil rights, but he made no promises. Neither man understood the other.

Daley did not understand King's goal of changing the system of discrimination. King did not understand white mayors who smiled and did nothing.

A day later someone turned on a fire hydrant in an effort to cool off from the heat. Police came to turn off the water, and a three-day riot was set off. The riot area covered 140 blocks. At night snipers attacked anyone on the street. It took four thousand National Guard troops to stop the riot.

When the riot ended, Mayor Daley, at King's insistence, launched a study to find ways to improve the relationship between Chicago's police and its black citizens. The mayor also had sprinklers installed on some fire hydrants and ordered above-ground swimming pools for some black areas.

The riot was a setback for King. The newspapers were filled with articles stating that Black Power leaders were winning the allegiance of black people. King, they said, might as well leave Chicago.

But King would not give up on Chicago. He set as his goal open housing for Chicago. The city should be a place where a person could live anywhere, regardless of his or her color. He led black marchers into the white suburbs of Chicago. In the Chicago Lawn neighborhood, the marchers were met by a hail of rocks, bottles, and firecrackers. "Two, four, six, eight! We don't want to integrate!" chanted some of the whites. They burned the cars the marchers had arrived in.

In Marquette Park, six thousand gathered to protest a black march through their neighborhood. Hurling bricks and shouting "Kill them! Kill them!" the whites transformed a pleasant suburban street into an alley of hate. Said King, "I have been in the civil rights movement for many years all through the South, but I have never seen mobs as hostile and hateful as this crowd."

Blacks without hope, whites full of hate, mayors who smiled politely and made no promises—this was the North. King was all but defeated by it. His ability to lead, his ideas for changing an unjust system were not working in Chicago.

As a southerner used to blatant racism, King found himself ill-equipped to deal with the subtle hypocrisy of northern racism. He simply had no ideas that could force the polite Daley to meet his demands. Daley unleashed no dogs nor did he call out the fire hoses. Rather, he smiled and ordered swimming pools—and still the unjust system of northern discrimination continued. If Daley, with his well-organized government, had a weakness that could be used against him, King could not find it. Boycotts of businesses in such a large city probably would not work. King was having trouble keeping his marchers nonviolent—thus large marches would not work. He was running out of ideas.

But he stayed.

And then there was Vietnam. As King continued to urge nonviolence, young black men would say, "What about Vietnam, that's violent?" King had to agree. Not only was the war violent but it was draining America of its spirit, its young men, and its resources.

He began to make speeches against the war. At Riverside Church in New York City, he said, "Somehow this madness must cease. . . . I speak as a child of God and brother to the suffering poor of Vietnam. I speak for those whose land is being laid waste, whose homes are being destroyed, whose culture is being subverted. I speak for the poor of America who are paying the double price of smashed hopes at home and death and corruption in Vietnam." In another speech, he pointed out that the United States "was spending an estimated $322,000 for each enemy we kill, while we spend in the so-called War on Poverty in America only about $53 for each person classified as poor."

King's stand on Vietnam did not win him many friends. In particular, he lost a very important friend in the White House. President Johnson had widened the war with the hope of winning it and instead found himself losing it. When King took his stand against U.S. involvement in Vietnam, he lost Johnson's firm support for his efforts.

Early in 1968 King began to plan a Poor People's Campaign. Groups of poor people in huge caravans would pour into Washington from the South, from Boston, Chicago, Newark, Pittsburgh, and many other cities. Once in Washington, they would remain there until Congress acted to meet their demands.

In the spring, he interrupted his plans for the Poor People's Campaign to go to Memphis. A minister had asked him to address a rally of striking garbage workers. The strike, which had begun as a union dispute, was six weeks old, and in recent days it had become violent. Most of Memphis' garbage workers were black, and the dispute had gradually widened into a civil rights conflict.

Speaking at the rally, King urged a one-day boycott of work for later in the month. "They will hear you, then," he promised. He came back to Memphis to lead the march. But the march deteriorated into a riot. It was learned that a group of teenagers had started the violence. King talked to them and exacted a promise that they would not make any trouble during the next march.

Early in April, when King returned to Memphis for the next march, he seemed troubled. Since the Montgomery bus boycott, he had received many threats on his life. But in the past few days, there had seemed to be more of them. In Memphis, the air was thick with whispered rumors that something was going to happen to him. At the rally that night he spoke of those threats. "Well, I don't know what will happen now. . . . Like anybody, I would like to live a long life. . . . But I'm not concerned about that now. I just want to do God's will. He's allowed me to go up to the mountain. And I've looked over, and I've seen the promised land."

The next day, April 4, as King left his motel room to go to dinner, he paused to lean over the balcony to talk to some friends in the courtyard below. Across the street, an assassin took aim and blasted away the help and the hope of thousands of black people. Martin Luther King, eyes wide open, lay on the floor of the balcony, bleeding from a huge neck wound. In minutes he was dead.

Across the street, James Earl Ray dropped his rifle and fled. Two months later Ray, an ex-convict, was captured by the FBI. He was later convicted of the crime. Ray claimed at his trial that he was a hired killer, part of a conspiracy.

King on the balcony of the Memphis hotel where
he was shot the next day. Next to King, tieless,
is Jesse Jackson. At right is Reverend Ralph
Abernathy; at left is Hosea Williams.

More than fifty thousand people marched in Martin Luther King, Jr.'s funeral procession through Atlanta on April 9, 1968.

King's death was a tragic loss. He had been a much loved husband, father, son, and brother. He had been a leader who could inspire. He had been, as the Nobel Prize committee had said, the one man in the Western world who had used nonviolence to right wrongs. But perhaps the greatest tragedy is that we will never know whether nonviolence might have worked to break the vicious cycle of poverty.

Messages of condolence came to the King family from all over the world, from the prime minister of India, from the pope, from the king of Sweden. President Johnson ordered the flag flown at half mast. The opening of the major league baseball season was postponed. The Academy Awards presentation was delayed.

His funeral was attended by the vice-president, senators, governors, mayors, entertainers, rabbis, bishops, and the ordinary people that he had tried to help. As the funeral ended, blacks and whites joined hands to sing "We Shall Overcome." Martin Luther King, Jr., would have been so pleased at the sight. It could never have happened without him.

EPILOGUE

Carved into the tombstone on King's grave are the words "Free At Last!"

It could be said that King was always free because he believed in himself and others, and because he was not afraid to stand up for what he thought was right. He was able to inspire these feelings in others.

"He had," said friend and advisor Bayard Rustin, "this tremendous facility for giving people the feeling they could be bigger and stronger and more courageous and more loving than they thought they could be."

People drew strength from King's words. They marched and they boycotted. They endured the fire hoses and the dogs. And the desegregation they achieved together remains today. "Whites only" signs are practically nonexistent. Blacks and whites share the same dining rooms, lodge in the same hotels, and share other public facilities.

Still, in many public places in the South, black people sense they are not welcome. But at least most white people now realize the injustice of segregation. For example, the "whites only" rule for membership in Birmingham, Alabama's Rotary

Club was recently abolished. "It made us all look a little silly that in 1982 people were still doing this," one member told *Newsweek* magazine. "Even George Wallace isn't talking that way anymore." Some members admitted privately to each other that they still believed in the "whites only" rule. But they were ashamed enough of the rule to vote against it.

Desegregation provided new opportunities for black people. As a result, the average income of the black family rose. In 1959, 48 percent of black families were poverty-stricken. By 1969, that number had dropped to 28 percent. The number of black-owned businesses rose steadily.

Desegregation in schools provided better educational opportunities for black people. By the 1980s the number of black college students had more than doubled.

The Voting Rights Act of 1965, inspired by the Selma campaign, resulted in an increase of black voter registration from two million to more than nine million. These black voters went to the polls and helped to push the number of black elected or appointed officials from four hundred to nearly six thousand. The cities of Gary, Indiana; Detroit; Newark, New Jersey; Los Angeles; Hartford, Connecticut; New Orleans; and even Birmingham and Atlanta elected black mayors.

In the seventies, the Vietnam War, recession, inflation, and oil-price increases began to sap the nation's dollar resources, cutting short the promise of King's triumphs. Even so, there were some gains. By 1978 the number of black people holding white-collar jobs had risen to 33 percent from 24 percent in 1970. And the number of blacks in professional and technical jobs also rose. However, by the end of the seventies, poverty had once again overwhelmed a large number of black families. As the eighties began, black unemployment was at a record high of 16 percent, more than twice that for whites. Most discouraging was the nearly 40 percent unemployment rate for teenagers, again twice the white rate. As recession and inflation ate away at the nation's resources, black ownership of urban and rural land dwindled.

Prodded by federal dollars and muscle, many white suburbs were integrated in the seventies. Money that might have gone to improve housing in the cities' slums was instead going to build housing for the poor in the suburbs. In the late seventies, whites beset by inflation and gasoline prices began moving back to the city from the suburbs. The freshly varnished doors and polished brass of renovated brownstones were the signs of well-to-do white people crowding poor black people out of run-down neighborhoods. Pressured by black lawmakers and leaders, the federal government agreed to relax a requirement that federally subsidized housing be built in integrated neighborhoods. And so in the eighties, black leaders made plans to use the allocated federal money to revitalize black slum communities.

Conservatives dominated the government in the late seventies and early eighties. In keeping with their political philosophy, they sought to institute the "New Federalism," which would "get the government off people's backs." These politicians wanted to return the administration of social programs such as education, nutrition, welfare, and job training to the separate states. Some saw this return to states rights as a threat to the civil rights of blacks. It had been the government that had stepped in during the sixties to order the integration of public facilities and the fair allocation of welfare money to black people as well as equal opportunity to apply for other public help. Without this federal supervision, some feared, the gains made by King and the people who marched with him could be wiped out. Black writer Frank Harris III, in an article in the *Hartford Courant*, said of the New Federalism—"Fifty states and fifty ways to discriminate."

In 1982 the Voting Rights Bill of 1965 came up in Congress for renewal. Conservatives launched an attack to cripple the bill that had produced such a dramatic increase in black voter registration. But led by the NAACP, white and black leaders soundly defeated this effort. The bill was extended for twenty-five more years. There were still eight and a half million unregistered black voters, and in many areas, registrars continued to make it difficult for black voters to register.

At the NAACP national meeting held in Boston in 1982,

NAACP executive director Benjamin Hooks called 1982 "the year of the ballot box." He then described the NAACP plans for a voter registration and voter education campaign focusing on 105 congressional districts. He pledged that black voters would join with women, labor, and Hispanic voters to defeat those conservative members of Congress who supported some of the New Federalism policies. Hooks criticized the "unfair tax cuts" which take money away from social programs in order to cut taxes for the rich. Such a program is not "anti-black, as such" but rather "anti-poor," said Hooks.

During the convention, word was received that the Supreme Court had approved the NAACP's right to boycott. Hooks announced that the NAACP would lead economic boycotts of those companies and industries that fail to give equal employment opportunities to black people.

A black minister closed the convention with a prayer of thanksgiving for the Supreme Court decision. "Thank the Lord," he prayed. "We're not going to let Martin Luther King down. . . . Let the world know our movement is God's movement. We shall overcome." The members stood and sang out "Amen!" and "Thank the Lord."

It was like the old days. But these were new days with new battles and new victories to pursue. The people had the courage to believe in themselves. King had helped them to find that. Surely they would overcome.

FOR
FURTHER
READING

Martin Luther King, Jr., wrote six books during his lifetime. Of special interest are *Stride Toward Freedom: The Montgomery Story* (New York: Harper & Row, 1958) and *Why We Can't Wait* (New York: Harper & Row, 1964). The latter is the story of the Birmingham campaign. Readers interested in learning more about King's philosophy should read *Strength to Love* (New York: Harper & Row, 1963).

Critical views of King can be found in *Martin Luther King, Jr.: A Profile*. Edited by C. Eric Lincoln (New York: Hill & Wang, 1970), the book contains essays about King by such people as Ralph Abernathy, Carl Rowan, David Halberstam, James Baldwin, and Lerone Bennett, Jr. *King: A Biography* by David L. Lewis (Urbana, Ill.: University of Illinois Press, 1978) is a balanced account of King that focuses on the significance of the events King lived. William Robert Miller's *Martin Luther King Jr.: His Life, Martyrdom and Meaning for the World* (New York: Weybright & Talley, 1968) is a more detailed account of King's life.

For a review of civil rights advances ten years after the 1963 March on Washington see the four-part series of articles which were published in *The New York Times*, August 27–30, 1973.

The seventieth anniversary issue (December 1980) of the National Association for the Advancement of Colored People (NAACP) periodical *The Crisis* is entirely devoted to the seventy years of progress in civil rights made since the founding of the organization. For more information about the 1982 voting and jobs campaign launched by the NAACP see *The Crisis*, February 1982.

INDEX

Lewis, John, 68–69
Lincoln Memorial, 37–38; 1963 March at, 66–71
Los Angeles, California, 108
Lunch counter segregation, 42–43

Malcolm X, 41
Maryland, 65
Mayors, black, 108
Michigan, 108
Mississippi, 41, 65
Montgomery, Alabama: bus boycott in, 3–15, 30–31, 35–36; 1961 riots in, 45–46; 1965 demonstrations at courthouse, 83–84
Montgomery Improvement Association (MIA), 7–14
Morehouse College, 25–28, 35

National Association for the Advancement of Colored People (NAACP), 4, 20, 30, 36, 109–110; early Atlanta chapter, 20–21
Nehru, Pandit, 40
New Federalism, 109–110
New Jersey, 108
New York, 65, 73
Newark, New Jersey, 108
1970s–1980s, black gains and losses in, 108–110
Nixon, E. D., 4, 5, 31
Nixon, Richard, 36, 37, 38, 39, 43
Nobel Peace Prize, 73
North Carolina, 42, 43
Northern cities, civil rights movement in, 65–71, 73, 96–102.

Parker, Mack, 41
Parks, Rosa, 3–7, 30–31
Peck, James, 45
Poor People's Campaign, 102–103
Project C, 52–53
Public Accomodations Act, 73

Randolph, A. Philip, 37, 66, 68
Ray, James Earl, 103
Recession, 108
Reeb, Reverend James J., 82
Rustin, Bayard, 66, 107

St. Augustine, Florida, civil rights campaign in, 71–73
School segregation, 41, 73, 97. See also Education
Segregation, 23–24; Birmingham, Alabama, 51–62; bus, 3–15, 30–31, 35–36, 46, 47, 52; church, 55; job, 47, 65, 96–97; lunch counter, 42–43; St. Augustine, Florida, 71–73; school, 41, 73, 97; Selma, Alabama, 77–87; sit-ins against, 42–45, 52–53; Supreme Court rulings on, 14, 30, 110; Watts, California, 91–95
Selma, Alabama, civil rights campaign in, 77–87
Shuttlesworth, Reverend Fred, 68
Sit-in movement, 42–45, 52–53
Slavery, 22, 27, 77
Southern Christian Leadership Conference (SCLC), 37, 38, 42–43, 45, 46, 52, 56, 58, 97
Southern cities. See names of cities
Spingarn Medal, 36
Stride Toward Freedom (King), 39
Student Nonviolent Coordinating Committee (SNCC), 43, 45, 100
Student sit-ins, 42–45
Supreme court rulings, 14, 110; Brown v. the Board of Education, 30

Thoreau, Henry, 26, 54
Transportation, segregated, 3–15, 25, 30–31, 46, 47, 52

Unemployment, 95–97, 100, 108

ABOUT THE AUTHOR

Jacqueline L. Harris, a writer and a former medical technolo-
gist, specializes in medical and scientific news, features, edi-
torials, and books for adults and young people. She is the
coauthor of another biography of Martin Luther King, Jr., and
of *Nine Black American Doctors* for young readers. Ms. Harris
received bachelors' degrees in bacteriology and journalism
from Ohio State University. She lives in Wethersfield, Connecticut.